Living
God's Politics

Living God's Politics

A Guide to Putting
Your Faith into Action

Jim Wallis

with Chuck Gutenson
and the editors of *Sojourners*

HarperSanFrancisco
A Division of HarperCollins*Publishers*

HarperCollins books may be purchased for educational, business, or sales promotional use. For information please write: Special Markets Department, HarperCollins Publishers, 10 East 53rd Street, New York, NY 10022.

HarperCollins Web site: http://www.harpercollins.com

HarperCollins®, ▲®, and HarperSanFrancisco™ are trademarks of Harper-Collins Publishers.

FIRST EDITION
Designed by Sharon VanLoozenoord

Library of Congress Cataloging-in-Publication Data

Wallis, Jim.
    Living God's politics : a guide to putting your faith into action / Jim Wallis ; with the editors of Sojourners magazine.—1st ed.
    p. cm.
    ISBN-10: 0–06–111841–9
    ISBN-13: 978–0–06–111841–8
    1. Christianity and politics—United States. 2. Christians—Political activity. I. Wallis, Jim. God's politics. II. Title.

BR526.W2655 2005
261.70973—dc22   2006043524

06 07 08 09 10 RRD(H) 10 9 8 7 6 5 4 3 2 1

Contents

vii   Introduction: Getting the Most from *Living God's Politics*

xi   Before You Start

1   *Week One:* Faith and Politics

15   *Week Two:* War and Peace

33   *Week Three:* Economic Justice

51   *Week Four:* Poverty

65   *Week Five:* A Consistent Ethic of Life

81   *Week Six:* Racism

99   *Week Seven:* Strengthening Family and Community Values

113   *Week Eight:* Hope for the Future

129   Appendix: A Summary of Social Activism Techniques

147   Getting Involved

153   Notes

157   Acknowledgments

Getting the Most from
Living God's Politics

WE ARE DELIGHTED that you are taking this opportunity to study *God's Politics* by Jim Wallis and to use this workbook as a way to more fully equip yourself to understand and live its message. *Living God's Politics* is not only a commentary on *God's Politics* (though it is that). Rather, *Living God's Politics* is intended to build upon the commitments presented in the book in three ways.

First, we provide resources and information aimed to help you probe more deeply into the major themes covered in *God's Politics (GP)*. Second, while it is important to understand the content of *GP*, it is more important to begin to live out its challenges in our daily lives. To that end, we have provided specific suggestions on a number of different activities that might enable you to act on the message of *GP*. At the end of the day, both *God's Politics* and *Living God's Politics (LGP)* are intended to help you think through what your faith means and to learn how that faith can be expressed in public life. *LGP* has been structured specifically for these purposes.

The material is arranged so that you might work through *LGP* and *GP* together over a period of eight weeks. Each week covers one theme from *GP*, and each day of a given week focuses on a particular aspect of that week's theme. In order to get the most from this study, we recommend that you gather together with others and undertake your reflections in a group setting. You could form a group from your congregation, school, organization, or other association. Either small groups or more formal Sunday school classes would provide excellent opportunities for community, fellowship, and study. In many cases, members of your group may choose to work together as you seek to study and act on your insights.

Second, we at Sojourners/Call to Renewal are constantly developing new resources and planning various ways to express a healthy and vibrant vision of faith in public life. We invite you to visit our Web sites (www.sojo.net and www.calltorenewal. org) to see the latest developments. In fact, when you visit our site, be sure to sign up for SojoMail, our weekly e-zine. (You can find it by going to www.sojo.net and clicking on SojoMail.) SojoMail is free, provides access to a wealth of resources and action ideas, and gives an entry into the Sojourners/Call to Renewal community.

Third, you can build on the material we present by making a firm commitment to each other for regular study and prayer as you work through *LGP* and *GP*.

It is our hope that the experience will be life-transforming for you and your study partners. However, for it to be so, you will need a core of firmly committed people who are passionate about hearing the full breadth of the biblical call to social justice and are willing to experiment with what they have heard. We encourage you and your group to consider establishing a covenant to read and be prepared for each week's study. Please go to the Sojourners Web site and use the "meet up" feature to locate other folks in your area who are interested in studying together. Let us know how your study is going.

Now let's take a look at the eight-week format. As noted, the study consists of weekly sessions built around the central themes addressed in *God's Politics*. Those themes and the order in which they will be covered are as follows:

Week One: Faith and Politics

Week Two: War and Peace

Week Three: Economic Justice

Week Four: Poverty

Week Five: A Consistent Ethic of Life

Week Six: Racism

Week Seven: Strengthening Family and Community Values

Week Eight: Hope for the Future

Each week is prefaced with the connection between *GP* and *LGP*. In particular, we will indicate the appropriate chapters from *GP* to read in conjunction with that week's theme. We will not repeat the content from those chapters, though we will provide a brief summary of each. Some chapters are used in more than one week. These introductions serve as the bridge between the workbook and the book. During the course of each week, specific aspects of the theme will be examined by means of a focused reading for each day of the week. The subtopics remain the same from week to week, as follows:

Day 1: Introducing the Topic

Day 2: Considering the Evidence

Day 3: Reading the Bible

Day 4: The Christian Tradition

Day 5: Living Examples in the Contemporary Church

Day 6: Putting Faith into Action

Day 7: Group Meeting and Reflection

Each week you and your group will consider one theme from *God's Politics* from a number of different perspectives. Some are aimed at providing a better grasp of the issue (Days 1 and 2); some at how Christians have thought about this issue (Days 3, 4, and 5), and one day each for considering specific ways that you might live out concern for that issue (Day 6) and for personal and group reflection (Day 7).

You can organize and schedule your group in any of a number of ways. However, we suggest that Day 7 would be the best day to meet as a group. By then you will have processed the week's material as individuals. Your group meeting will allow you to consider the issue together using the suggested questions and discuss each other's personal reflections. It is important that your discussion explicitly consider the focus of Day 6. Of course, you should feel free to creatively move beyond the suggestions that we have included. Look for opportunities to select actions that meet the needs of your particular community. Don't feel discouraged if you are unable to plan an action item with regard to each and every theme. However, strategically choosing ways you will act on what you are learning is critical to the study. So even if you cannot engage in some activity from Day 6 each week, consider selecting a subset of the themes on which to undertake particular actions.

The appendix to this book provides a number of ideas on how to engage in different kinds of social action, from letter-writing campaigns to educational events to community organizing to demonstrations to nonviolent civil disobedience. Some forms of social action fit better than others with particular themes we will study together. In our material for Day 6 of each week, we have listed brief examples of the kinds of social action we see as best fitting each theme. To avoid repetition, however, we have provided the details in the appendix. As noted above, please feel free to step outside the box and come up with your own creative ways to act on *God's Politics*.

Once again, welcome to this study! It is our prayer that God's Spirit will be active in your life as you seek to live out the biblical call to justice and love.

Before You Start

AS YOU PREPARE to work through *God's Politics* with *Living God's Politics* as a guide, take a few minutes to prepare yourself by recording your current thoughts on several questions. Reflect, either individually or with your study group, on the following:

1. Before you begin to read through *God's Politics* and *Living God's Politics*, consider what you think of the relation between faith and politics—particularly how faith should inform and guide us on political issues. Does God have a "politics"? Why do you say this?

2. Construct a list of factors that you think must be taken into consideration when developing commitments that adequately reflect God's intentions for our public life together. In other words, how would a society that lives according to God's intention that we work for the common good be organized and structured? What kinds of public and social institutions would it have? What would its priorities be?

3. What point is *God's Politics* trying to make with the subtitle "Why the Right Gets It Wrong and the Left Doesn't Get It"? As you read through the book, develop a list of things you would say to the Right and then to the Left if you were given an opportunity to address them. Be sure to defend your list from a faith perspective.

Take notes on your reflections so you will have them available after the study in order to assess whether and how your thinking has changed. At the end, we will return to a similar set of questions. Enjoy your study! Now on to Week 1.

Living
God's Politics

Faith and Politics

THE TOPIC FOR this first section is the relationship between faith and politics. This theme relates particularly to the introduction of *God's Politics* as well as to chapters 1 to 3, 5, and 6. Chapter 4 is related as well, and it will also be associated later (along with chapter 6) with the concluding theme of hope. Be sure to review chapters 1 to 3, 5, and 6 during the course of working through this first section of *Living God's Politics*. The following paragraphs provide a brief overview of each of those chapters.

Introduction: Since politics is ultimately about ordering our communal life together, it is far too important an aspect of human life to be considered outside of God's care and attention. God has a "political perspective," one might say, rooted in God's identity as Creator and expressed in the Bible. However, God's politics always challenges our politics. We too easily pursue ideological agendas that serve our own interest. God's politics is never ideological, but always intends to benefit human well-being. In particular, God reminds us of our obligations to the persons we often neglect—the poor, the vulnerable, and those otherwise on the margins. God's politics challenges both the political Left and the political Right to offer a new vision of faith and politics, a vision more in line with God's intentions and the common good.

Chapter 1: Many people feel that there is no political option that does justice to their understanding of the Christian faith. They feel that Christian language has been co-opted by the Right and used to accomplish ends that are not consistent with a full expression of the faith they hold. Likewise, they feel that the Left has tended to treat them as if their faith were irrelevant for political life. These folks long for a return to a genuine faith that transcends these options. They embrace a faith that unapologetically engages the public political discourse while insisting upon a moral vision consistent with that taught and lived by Jesus and the biblical prophets.

Chapter 2: "Without vision the people perish" (Proverbs 29:18). This ancient biblical proverb actually makes one point, but it implies an equally important second point. On the first, it is clear from history that where ambiguity and confusion are evident and there is an absence of vision, the people suffer. Without vision, there is no "road map" to a better tomorrow. On the second point, the people also suffer where there is wrong or misguided vision. When you are going in the wrong direction, "making progress" is not a virtue. Now is the time to develop an alternative vision for the intersection of religious and public life and to call public institutions to accountability for how well they serve the common good, rather than the good of special interest groups.

Chapter 3: To suggest that God is concerned only with our private lives implies a "household god"—a god who watches over our private piety but cares little about public life. Such a god is not the God of the Judeo-Christian heritage. God is deeply personal and is clearly concerned about our personal morality. However, even a quick read through the Bible reveals a God who is also very interested in the shape of our social values and public life. In particular, God is concerned that public institutions prevent the exploitation of society's most marginalized persons. God gives commands aimed at preventing such exploitation, and those passages dealing with divine judgment make it clear that God takes very seriously the extent to which our public life includes those concerns for justice.

Chapter 5: At its worst, religious fundamentalism seeks political power to impose a theocracy; secular fundamentalism, on the other hand, attempts to confine religious faith only to private expression or houses of worship. The real question is not whether religious faith should influence a society and its politics, but rather how: What form of influence would be most consistent with our faith and provide the best opportunity to positively impact our culture? For example, the religious Right that emerged in the 1980s preferred a more partisan approach, seeking to gain control of the levers of power in order to enact change. The civil rights movement, on the other hand, was more morally based and politically independent, seeking to motivate change from the outside.

Chapter 6: There are three dominant political options in America. One is conservative on everything—from cultural and family concerns to economic and foreign policy issues. The second is liberal on everything across the same spectrum. The third is libertarian—liberal on cultural/family issues and conservative on fiscal/economic policy. A fourth option, one that is largely missing within the current American political scene, is traditional or conservative on issues of family values and sexual integrity, for example, while progressive or populist on issues of economic justice and peacemaking. Some are beginning to see the false dichotomy embodied by viewing everything as either liberal or conservative, and Christians have an opportunity to lead a significant change in the political landscape of this country.

DAY 1 — Introducing the Topic

Early on, *God's Politics* makes the claim that "God is personal, but never private." In fact, *God's Politics* emphasizes that point by making it the subtitle to the third chapter. It is a point that is far more important than is often realized. While on the one hand God cannot somehow be relegated merely to the nonpublic areas of our lives, on the other hand God must be understood as also concerned with the personal aspects of our lives.

Central to the Christian faith is the idea that God is not a remote, uncaring, impersonal God, but rather is fully engaged and interactive with creation. But what does it mean to affirm that God is personal? Well, first and foremost, to be a person is to be in relation with others. In other words, the basic idea behind the term "person" is not that of a lone individual, but rather of an individual who stands among and in relation to others. Obviously, we do not cease being persons when we are alone; however, who we are as persons is built from our relationships with one another. We are who we are precisely as a consequence of the various relations we have had with other persons over time. If those relationships had been different, we would, in a very real sense, be different people. To be a person is to be in relation with others, and for the Christian, those others include God and the rest of creation.

Christian ethicist Stanley Hauerwas once said that the Bible is not so much a book about what we ought to do as it is a book about who God is, and what we ought to do flows from that knowledge. We have been created so that relationships, both with God and with the rest of creation, are a major factor in forming us as specific persons. All of us bear the marks of our various relationships, and this is a powerful reminder of how much God intends us to impact each other for the better.

To claim that God is always personal, then, is important at several different levels. First, it affirms the reality that God is not distant and uncaring. Rather, God desires a deeply personal relationship with each and every one of us. Second, it affirms the deeply community-oriented "way of being" that God intends for us and that we embody when we enter into loving relationships with those around us. In short, we realize our personhood as God intended it to be when we love God with our whole hearts and our neighbors as ourselves. Robert Mulholland, professor of New Testament at Asbury Seminary, emphasizes the close connection between these two great commands by translating them (roughly): Love the Lord your God with all your heart, mind, soul, and strength, and *another way of saying the same thing,* love your neighbor as yourself. When we combine these two points, we see that God is intensely concerned about our personal moral and spiritual growth. What we must not miss is that, because of the way that God has created us to be persons in relationship, God is equally concerned about how we organize ourselves into communities and the social structures and rules that organize our common life.

The second part of the claim from *God's Politics* is that "God is never private." For Christians, there is a sense in which everything changed with the life of Jesus. With his exemplary life, death, and resurrection, a new order has been ushered into existence. The essential affirmation of the post-Easter period is that "Jesus is Lord." Unfortunately, in our contemporary setting, this affirmation has lost some of its force. It is often reduced to little more than a statement about personal piety; that is, we live as if the affirmation were "Jesus is Lord of my private life." This is true enough, but to limit Jesus's primacy to our private lives is to miss the biblical claim that Jesus is now Lord over all creation, personal and communal, private and public. If we claim the primacy of Jesus as Christ, then we cannot worship idols or allow any other political or religious leaders to make claims on our faith—a faith that belongs to God alone. Christians need to recapture the boldness of the biblical vision for our communities and public institutions that flows from a fuller realization of the vision of Jesus.

If we fail to see God's personal nature, we will miss the importance God places upon our development into the persons we ought to be. We will also miss the extent to which God intends our character to be worked out within community. In turn, this will lead us to miss the extent to which God cares about the manner in which we organize our social life and communities and structure them so as to allow for the flourishing of all God's children. As *God's Politics* points out, the Hebrew prophets did not miss either of these points in their critiques. It is worth reflecting on how the prophets Amos or Isaiah might speak God's truth to power structures in our contemporary setting. Without an adequate sense of the implications of the relationship between God and creation, we miss the fact that God cares about the nature of the institutions we establish in our communal (that is, public) everyday lives. A great danger is the tendency to conceive of God and God's concerns as merely private matters.

All of this means, then, that Christians must prayerfully examine the Bible and the history of the church to be certain that the social life we establish adequately addresses the issues that God expresses most concern about. These issues include personal morality (sexual integrity, for example) as well as public morality (the community's obligation to care for "the least of these," for example). Neither alone is adequate.

We often hear those on the political Right argue that concern for the poor is valid but that such concerns are to be addressed on the personal level, either by persons or by churches, but not by governments. This is a much too anemic view of God's concerns. Public policies, priorities, and programs are all part of the system established to organize our shared lives. For Christians, this means arguing for policies, priorities, and programs that defend and protect "the least of these." An attitude of "each one on his or her own" will not pass biblical muster.

The implications this has for Christian life are remarkable. For example, conventional wisdom has it that two subjects forbidden from polite conversation are religion and politics. Yet it is hard to imagine two subjects of more consequence for day-to-day human life. Perhaps we need to learn a new sort of civility that will allow us vigorously to engage each other, seeking to come to a better consensus about realizing God's intentions in our public life.

In conclusion, let us remember that God is always personal and never private, which means that God is interested in human life and in moral choices at all levels, from the personal to the church to the local community to the nation and, finally, to the entire world.

DAY 2 — Considering the Evidence

Imagine you are a person deeply mired in catastrophic poverty, a member of an ethnic minority concerned about workplace protections, or a person with an illness for which treatment would be long and expensive. Or imagine you are a member of the solid middle class worried about the demise of the middle class. Or that you are reasonably well off and hoping to ... well, stay well off. In each of these cases, you are imagining yourself as a person with deep and serious concerns related to your well-being and that of the society in which you live. Now imagine that someone said to you that you should not bring these concerns with you as you participate in public political dialogue. Would that make sense?

In a similar fashion, many persons of deep religious faith find it hard to imagine why the factor that most constitutes who they are and guides their political and economic choices—their faith in God—should be set aside from public discussion. For many, the separation of faith and society (as distinct from the separation of church and state) is not simply mistaken, it is impossible. If one takes following Jesus to be the very core of Christian faith, then one cannot leave that behind when dealing with public policies and institutions.

Now, it is important to clarify that engaging politics from the perspective of faith does not mean violating the separation of church and state. In fact, quite the opposite. Even a quick review of the history of the church shows that persons of faith are pretty much as likely as other groups to exploit political power when they hold it. For example, when religious groups move from one region to avoid religious persecution, they often end up persecuting the nonreligious in their new region once they gain power. So the separation of church and state, which ensures that no one particular religion becomes the official state religion, is critical to a healthy democracy. While few religious groups claim openly that they want to form a state church, as we see in history these things have a way of "just happening."

There is no reason, however, that affirming the basic rightness of church-state separation has to mean excluding persons of faith from the public debate over social policy and the direction of public institutions. Nor must persons of faith feel it inappropriate to utilize the insights they gain from their religious traditions in forming their moral compass on policy matters. However, it would not be appropriate for people of religious faith to argue for nondemocratic policies or for exclusion or inclusion of others on the basis of religion. As long as individuals remain free to use their faith in their decision making, a healthy sense of a separation of the state from favoring any particular church or religious movement is not at all inconsistent with bringing one's faith to bear on social and political matters.

The next question one must consider is the form that participation should take. Perhaps one of the greatest temptations for those who participate in the political process is the ease with which one gets drawn into the "power game." After all, if one has strong commitments, then there is a great temptation to see one's political connections as a means to grasp the reins of control in order to bring into reality the perceived better way of being that arises from one's faith commitments. This is what German philosopher Friedrich Nietzsche called the "will to power"—the deep-seated need to exert our will over others. When we find ourselves in positions of power and authority, it is easy for the pursuit of power to be self-confirming in our own minds. Why would God have allowed us to take power if we were not fully equipped to use it? This can be a slippery, arrogant, and terribly dangerous slope.

Another role that people of faith have sometimes been drawn into is that of chaplain to the state, a sort of religious courtesan. The courts of power do not like to be challenged, and remaining close to them often means giving up the ability to be prophetic and to speak truth to power. People thus co-opted are sometimes reduced to keeping the peace between the exploiters and the exploited, instead of standing up for those victimized by the powerful.

How does a person maintain a prophetic stance that "speaks truth to power"? The prophetic task involves both *modeling* what God intends and *speaking out* for policies and institutions that support the biblical mandates for peace with justice. People of faith, and the church as a whole, have made important political and social contributions in the United States.

The abolition of slavery, the fight for women's suffrage, the passage of child labor laws, and the advocacy for civil rights are a few of the movements driven by people of faith because of their religious convictions. The method used by Martin Luther King Jr.—engaging the powers without becoming one of them—is an example of how the church should challenge and engage unjust political institutions. King wrote that the church is to be neither master nor servant of the state, but rather its conscience—that is, to be prophetic.

DAY 3

Reading the Bible

There is little debate among Christians today over the claim that God has specific expectations for the moral conduct of our personal lives. What is sometimes missed is that there are serious implications for our public life together that flow directly from our faith in Christ. Today, we examine the Bible to explore how

God's moral expectations of us as persons in relation with God and with the rest of creation inform both our individual conduct as well as our public conduct.

That God has expectations for us is immediately clear from the creation accounts themselves. There we are told that God entrusts Adam and Eve with care for the Garden of Eden, and ultimately, for the earth. By the time we get to the story of Noah, we find that humanity has become so evil that God destroys the earth and starts again. Later, we come to the explicit statement of the kinds of expectations God has with the instruction to the people at Mt. Sinai—the Ten Commandments. The commandments divide into two sets: (1) those dealing with the relationship between God and humanity and (2) those dealing with the relationship between and among humans. In essence, we are to honor God and our fellow creatures. The commandments take specific form in declaring idolatry and the misuse of God's name as immoral, and they also identify the immorality of stealing, adultery, lying, and longing for the possessions of others. Despite broad consensus among Christians and much of the larger population over these personal edicts, the public side of what it means to be a person in relation with God and the rest of creation is often more disputed.

We frequently hear it claimed that Jesus was not interested in politics. Perhaps this error arises from too narrow a description of the term "politics." The term comes from the Greek word "polis," which simply means "city." So, the term "politics" in its most general sense is not about the endless debates between political parties, but rather about the manner in which human societies are to be organized. To think that Jesus had no interest in this sense of politics makes a division between private and public that is a contemporary invention, one that is justified by neither the Bible nor church history.

For example, in Luke 4:18, when Jesus stands in the synagogue and announces his ministry—"The Spirit of the Lord is upon me, because he has anointed me to bring good news to the poor"—his language is from the Hebrew prophets who proclaimed God's intentions regarding the sorts of characteristics our shared lives should exhibit. All of life is to reflect the divine intent: to care for the marginalized and the sick and to welcome the stranger. It would be strange indeed for Jesus to consistently teach and live these themes in the scriptures but somehow intend them for only the private realm. If anything, Jesus expands and deepens our obligations, both individually and corporately.

Perhaps one of the most powerful summaries of the reality of God's intentions across all levels of human life is expressed in Paul's letter to the Colossians. Here we are told that "in him [Jesus] all things were created, in heaven and on earth, visible and invisible, whether thrones or dominions or principalities or authorities—all things were created through him and for him" (Colossians 1:16). In other words, there is no power of government or public institutions that is beyond Christ's authority. Public institutions, whatever form they take, are subject to the ethics of peace, justice, and care for the least of these that God mandates. The values—implicit and explicit—in Jesus's teachings should be central to our understanding of their right role in ordering our lives together.

Romans 13 is sometimes cited in discussions about the role of public institutions, but too often it is separated from the teachings in Romans 12. In Romans 12, Paul lays out what our life together should look like. Then, in Romans 13, he presents an affirmation of public institutions that realize the sorts of common, public life that would follow from the exhortations of Romans 12. To read chapter 13 as some sort of carte blanche for public officials would be to forget the preceding chapter. More obviously, it would overlook the fact that Paul was, himself, later executed by the state.

The point is straightforward. God cares about the nature and characteristics of our lives—both our personal lives and our public institutions. We are called to do what we can to shape public institutions and what they do. We should strive for public institutions that reflect God's intentions.

DAY 4 — The Christian Tradition

The early Christians did not openly participate in the mechanisms of the state. In the first three centuries, church leaders were overwhelmingly opposed to participation in the military. In fact, the early church often found itself on the receiving end of abuse from the Roman Empire. Christians were sacrificed in the "gladiator sport," fed to lions for the sick amusement of others. When the Roman Empire collapsed, some blamed the early Christians, who were charged with an atheism characterized not by the rejection of any concept of God, but rather by the rejection of the pagan "gods" of Rome—a charge that prompted Augustine to write in defense of Christianity. Given that milieu, the reticence of early Christians toward political entities is certainly understandable.

Due to these hostilities, there was little opportunity for direct involvement by early Christians in the formal political process. This, however, did not preclude Christians from offering a critique from outside the corridors of power—indeed, they frequently had comments to make about the political situation. In the heyday of the Roman Empire, the emperor was understood to be divine, and citizens of the empire were expected to affirm that Caesar was lord. This presented a problem, because of course the early church was centered on its affirmation that Jesus was Lord. The direct implication of affirming the lordship of Jesus was the denial of the lordship of Caesar. There was a direct correspondence between the life of faith and political life. In fact, the two were so intertwined that Caesar could not allow his authority to be challenged by those placing the authority of Jesus over his own. Those who openly claimed Jesus as Lord were often killed. A merely "private" faith, on the other hand, would not have been perceived as a threat by Rome.

When Emperor Constantine legalized Christianity in the empire, much of this tension changed. In what many view as a compromise with the empire, Christians were now viewed more favorably. Christian thinkers began to address openly the vexing questions of how the life of faith and the political life are related. Augustine formulated a position that made explicit the distinction between church and state by writing about two "cities": the city of God (characterizing the life of faith and its end in heaven) and the city of "man" (characterizing human life and its management).

From these early writings developed the doctrine of the "two kingdoms," which Martin Luther later expounded upon. The first was described as the earthly kingdom presided over by the relevant political powers. The second was the heavenly kingdom, or the kingdom of faith, ultimately presided over by God but watched over on earth by the church. Augustine had a significant impact on the way the church tended to think of the intersection of faith and politics.

This dichotomy led some to understand that faith is to be lived out only in private and that the public management of human societies is to be undertaken by secular authorities. The work of Augustine, however, did not intend this conclusion. When the Roman Empire collapsed, the church quite willingly moved in and assumed "secular" authority.

Through history Christianity has had various relationships with the state: it has been persecuted by the state; it has operated as the primary power over government when there has been a state religion; and it has acted as a prophetic corrective to the state, while maintaining a separation that allows for religious diversity. In a participatory democracy, the best interest of the country is served when religion appeals to the common good from consistent moral grounds. It was from those grounds that Martin Luther King Jr. and the civil rights movement changed America.

DAY 5 — Living Examples in the Contemporary Church

When we think of the engagement of faith and politics, the temptation is to think of something big, something of international significance. Most of what we hear on the evening news relates to matters that capture national attention. However, if we dismiss local concerns, then many of us would rarely find opportunities to live our faith in political action. What are the opportunities for living our faith on the local level?

A Lexington, Kentucky, group known as Communality, part of the burgeoning house church movement, helps show us the way. Communality meets in small groups in homes; members enjoy a meal together, then engage in worship and discussion.

They invite any and all comers to share dinner and time together with them. They describe themselves as a group of Christians putting "skin on the missional church." They host presentations on various social justice topics and are always on the lookout for ways to live out their faith by caring for "the least of these."

I'VE SEEN THE MOUNTAINTOP . . . REMOVED

Sometime back in 2004, a Christian group called Communality became aware of an issue known as "mountaintop removal." This procedure was begun by the coal companies as a less expensive way to remove coal from deep within the mountains of West Virginia, as well as in the states where rich coal reserves are hidden inside ancient formations.

Mountaintop removal is just as it sounds—the coal company quite literally blows the top off of a mountain. As you can imagine, this creates massive problems for the area's residents. One West Virginian described living near the mountains as feeling like he was "in the middle of a war zone." To achieve the necessary removal of the top of a mountain, hundreds of thousands of tons of dynamite are used. But worse than the sound is the sediment. What can be done with thousands of tons of rock? The coal companies dump it into the valleys below. This, plus the loss of ground cover, often leads to massive flooding in the valleys below the coal operations.

There are many other issues involved. The huge trucks carrying the coal create ruts so deep that cars can no longer go down certain roads. And one mother described the anguish she felt from the fact that the water had turned so brown due to runoff that she could no longer bathe her daughter.

Still, all of this occurs hundreds of miles away from Lexington. Why should a group of Christians living in the city care about the mountains? As Communality became aware of the issue, they started asking the same question. But one of the deep values of the community is the interconnected nature of life. They believe that what happens in the hills of West Virginia has significant impact on the lives of people living in cities far away. Matters of injustice in one place have a way of spreading injustice all around. People were suffering from this problem while city folks enjoyed the benefits of cheaper energy that results from this procedure. Communality members felt compelled to action.

Not many U.S. Christians have paid much attention to this issue. Allen Johnson and Christians for the Mountains (www.christiansforthemountains.org) have been among the few voices within the church seeking justice in this area. So as they got involved, many of the relationships they began to develop were outside of the faith community. Some environmental groups were decidedly anti-faith.

Communality offered one of the best resources they had available to the environmentalists—space. They had a community house in the city, and a number of groups had banded together to seek to raise awareness on the issue. This gave Communality a point of interaction. They fed the activists. They housed them. Relationships developed that would never have existed otherwise.

Communality has been involved in other ways, including helping to promote an educational campaign and going to the mountains to observe the suffering firsthand. But perhaps their greatest contribution is relationship. By being willing to enter into friendship with those who are active in key issues, they are living out the Christian story.

WILL SAMSON*

Where will the efforts of Communality lead them? No one knows, of course, but in their effort to speak for those residents of communities threatened by the practice of mountaintop removal, they made new friends. In addition to those they sought to defend, some of the environmental groups were able to see Christian faith in a new light. Rather than being offended at what Samson calls an "anti-faith" position, the members of Communality looked past this bias in search of dialogue. Their efforts were rewarded. They gained colleagues with whom to work for social justice in the area of mining and corporate accountability.

What are the parallel concerns in your area, and how might you forge alliances to combat the injustices?

DAY 6   Putting Faith into Action

As noted earlier, many have observed that religion and politics seem to be the two subjects that are not to be engaged in public conversation. Why is this? It is hard to imagine two things more important than these in determining the shape and form of our communities and our shared lives. Persons of faith are formed by their religious beliefs, and religious belief deals intimately with how we live together in community. An important two-part question, then, is, What kind of community does our faith call us to, and how should our social and political institutions be structured to make that a reality?

Perhaps the most important thing that we can do to integrate our faith and our politics is to change the perception that faith and politics should not be discussed in polite company. This means seeking to engage our fellow believers on political matters, not just for the sake of debate, but rather to see how our faith informs our political commitments. If we carry on this discussion politely, but passionately, we should be able to succeed in demonstrating that this important dialogue can be undertaken both amicably and seriously.

From the list of potential activities in the appendix, there are several that could be used to explore this issue. We suspect that the sort of movement we have suggested begins with education. Some excellent starting points would include preparing a course of study or outlining a series of sermons for your local church. Provide both

---

* *Will Samson is a student at Asbury Theological Seminary in Wilmore, Kentucky.*

a biblical and a theological basis for teaching people how to connect their faith commitments and particular political visions with action. Primarily, your goal is to create an environment that is conducive to dialogue on faith and politics. This environment should not only tolerate but actually welcome varying opinions and points of view.

Also, look for opportunities to broaden the public discourse. Write letters to the editor of local newspapers. Offer opinion pieces. Call in to radio talk shows. Get involved in key local, national, and global issues. Every other year is an election year in the United States. Use this rhythm to create a calendar for your teaching series. In the off-years, offer general studies about the relation between faith and politics and studies on the biblical role of government. In election years, assuming this background has been provided, focus on electoral issues and ballot initiatives. (Of course, if you do so on behalf of a church or other nonprofit group, make sure to do it in a nonpartisan manner.)

There are two very specific ways to influence positively the relationship between politics and religion. First, *God's Politics* argues that we must not allow ourselves to be forced to narrow our conception of biblical morality. It is common in our contemporary situation for politicians to employ "divide and conquer" strategies when it comes to influencing religious voters. To avoid this, we need a broader vision of biblical morality that moves beyond so-called wedge issues to insist that the Bible requires us to address a whole range of issues.

Second, we must be attentive to opportunities to work together on areas of common concern. While people on the extremes of the political spectrum might have a hard time finding agreement on issues, most people are in the broad political middle and can find common ground on many individual issues. Often we are divided by our methods more than by our goals. We can agree that poverty should be alleviated or abortions reduced, so how might we work on these issues together? When religious folks on both sides of the political spectrum stand up to speak with a unified voice to the corridors of power, political leaders begin to listen. *God's Politics* makes this point nicely: "Couldn't both pro-life and pro-choice political leaders agree to common ground actions that would actually reduce the abortion rate, rather than continue to use abortion mostly as a political symbol?"

DAY 7 — Group Meeting and Reflection

1. Discuss the extent to which religion and politics are intimately related. What evidence from the Bible or Christian tradition would you cite to support the relationship between the two?

2. Is it appropriate to think that God has a perspective on politics? To adequately reflect on this question, define the term "politics" from what you see

as a Christian perspective, show where that definition connects with Christian faith, and then discuss what it might mean to think of God as having a political perspective.

3. What are the implications of the title of *God's Politics*? What would it mean to affirm that God holds "political" commitments? As you read through the book, keep paper and pencil handy and try to outline the set of commitments God might have if this presentation is correct.

4. What is meant by the affirmation that God is personal, but never private? What implications would this have for how we think of political responsibilities?

5. On pages xxii through xxiv of *God's Politics*, the content of the "God Is Not a Republican ... or a Democrat" ad is presented. Review it and discuss your agreement or disagreement. Be sure to provide a basis for your rationale, preferably from within the religious tradition. Would this list make a useful guide for evaluating different political candidates? Why or why not?

6. Not many politicians would suggest that their faith leads them to be "pro-war," "pro-rich," and only "pro-American." Why would *God's Politics* suggest that, in practice, many U.S. politicians are asserting exactly that? How would you assess their claim?

7. *God's Politics* notes that "religious action is rooted in a much deeper place than 'rights'—that place being the image of God in every human being" (page 5). Reflect upon and discuss how this impacts our political commitments.

8. Assume you have a five-minute audience with the leadership of the current administration. What would you say in those five minutes to present a serious Christian political and moral agenda?

9. For a political vision to be moral and Christian, what are the elements that it must include? (Don't look for specific policy content here. Rather, think about what principles would guide the selection of policy content.)

10. Make a list of the ten political issues you would consider most relevant for persons of faith. How would you prioritize them based upon your faith? Why?

War and Peace

AS WE MOVE to Week 2, our topic changes from the relation between faith and politics in general to Christian attitudes toward war. This topic is covered in chapters 7 through 12 of *God's Politics*. In Days 1 and 2 of this week, we will focus on the war in Iraq, about which we know more now than when *God's Politics* was written. Be sure to review chapters 7 through 12 in *God's Politics* in preparation for this week's study.

The following is a summary of those chapters.

Chapter 7: Bad decisions too frequently arise out of fear—fear for our families, for ourselves, for our property. When we are fearful, we are ripe for manipulation by those who promise that, if only we will trust them, they will keep us safe. The terrorist attacks of September 11, 2001, changed our lives. As is often the case, the fear created by these attacks led us to accept policies that offered to reverse our newfound vulnerability. It is essential, however, that as Christians we take a step back from our fear, remembering who it is we ultimately trust, and ask the harder questions aimed at getting to the roots of terrorism. That will help us offer a better response than those that spring only from fear.

Chapter 8: Today, the primary positions that Christians hold with regard to war include the "just war" theory, active nonviolence, and pacifism. (The latter two are often lumped together.) In Iraq, it was clear that Saddam Hussein was a terrible dictator, and removing him from power was a desirable goal. But was that enough to justify the U.S. invasion of Iraq? In fact, no form of the just war theory allows for "preemptive" war-making such as the U.S. attack against Iraq. We have learned in the past few years that virtually all the intelligence used in the run-up to the war was at best mistaken or at worst manipulated. Ironically, the nature of the war and how it was sold to the American public has actually weakened our ability to combat genuine threats of terrorism.

Chapter 9: History teaches us that few things are more dangerous than the potent combination of religious fervor and nationalistic zeal. The temptation to appeal to God to further our own interest is a blatant misuse of religion. Yet such appeals are too often made from all sides of the political spectrum. Our fears cloud our judgment, and we become ensnared in the civil religion that arises from the marriage of God with national interests and agendas. We are vulnerable to embracing actions and policies that we normally would never consider. As British historian Lord Acton observed, "Power tends to corrupt; absolute power corrupts absolutely." That observation seems to hold true for countries as well as individuals. Being the world's only "superpower" seems to have had a negative effect on the United States' ability to conduct foreign policy in an ethical manner consistent with international law.

The word "empire" has been used by senior Bush advisers[1] (and others) to describe American power in the world, and the concept is often defended by the president, even using religious language. But in biblical terms, religious nationalism is a form of idolatry, and as such it must be resisted by people of faith.

Chapter 10: Unfortunately, it is too often the case that people don't begin to ask questions about peacemaking until a crisis point is reached—or worse, until after hostilities have begun. Genuine peacemaking, however, recognizes that conflict can occur any time there is a human encounter, and it seeks proactively to sow the seeds of peace prior to crisis.

The realities of war justify the claim that "war is hell." It is important to keep these realities in mind as we seek to find creative ways to resolve conflict and reduce violence. An important part of peacemaking is the willingness to look below the surface, to locate the presence of injustices that have the potential to foster hostility. By addressing and defusing the underlying causes, peacemakers can actually work against war before it starts. Even when a crisis is upon us, however, we must first look for nonviolent ways to respond.

Chapter 11: A resolution to the conflict between the Israelis and the Palestinians would be a huge step toward regional and even global peace. At the same time, the long history of animosity between the two sides makes people wonder whether a lasting peace with justice can ever be found. Any step forward, however, must begin with truth-telling. For example, while U.S. media have paid significant attention to Palestinian violence against Israelis, much less notice has been given to Israeli violence against Palestinians. Once the truth is told with impartiality, the international community will need to adopt an evenhanded strategy toward the legitimate rights and aspirations of both groups for security and self-determination.

Chapter Twelve: Genuine, lasting peace can only be based upon a real sense of security, which includes aspects that are personal, national, and global. Real security means, among other things, the assurance that all people have access to the essentials of life—such as adequate food, water, and housing. The prophet Micah offers a vision of the world where swords are beaten into plowshares and where nations do not make war against other nations. He goes on to envision everyone having their own "vine and fig tree," living free and unafraid. In short, a secure future will require dealing with causes and not merely symptoms.

Introducing the Topic

The Christian church historically has held three positions regarding war. For the first 300 years of the church, most Christians rejected war—and participation in Caesar's armies—as inconsistent with Christian faith. The majority of Christians in the early church took quite seriously Jesus's imperative to "love your enemies" and "resist not evil with evil." Some even accepted martyrdom rather than kill others in war. Beginning in the fourth and fifth centuries, primarily through the writing of Augustine, the church began to develop what became known as the "just war" theory, which claims that under certain conditions Christians can participate in warfare. During the Middle Ages, the church actually encouraged warring for certain "holy causes," and the result was the notion of war as crusade, a position that is now almost universally rejected.

Christian rejection of war, such as that practiced since the earliest days of the church, is often given the label of "pacifism," and many times the position is mischaracterized as Christian "passivism"—implying that the tactic is withdrawal and nonengagement. Christian peacemakers do not and cannot argue for "doing nothing." Instead, they argue that Christians are called to reject the use of lethal force, in war or elsewhere.

But the positive, peacemaking actions proposed and carried out by those rooted in the church's peace tradition are often ignored, belittled as unrealistic, or overlooked. This often results in peacemakers being asked at the last minute, when hostilities are imminent, "So, what do we do now? Nothing?" When this happens, the Christian peacemaking position is distorted into a purely reactive one, where the concern for peace is raised only at the verge of war. Instead, Christian peacemakers argue that one must engage in serious peacemaking activities long before the outbreak of war. Peacemaking requires vision, persistence, and a proactive engagement with the root causes of war and injustice. Ronald J. Sider's *Non-Violence: The Invincible Weapon?* and Peter Ackerman and Jack DuVall's *A Force More Powerful* (both the book and film) are excellent resources that outline successful cases of the use of nonviolent resistance in the face of aggression. There are many successful examples of nonviolence in action, including conflict resolution, and the church should work to teach each generation how to build on these successes and reclaim the tradition of Christian peacemaking to deal with conflict, oppression, and violence.

Despite Christianity's early understanding of the biblical call to peacemaking, by the fourth century the church's position began to change. In 312, the Roman general Constantine became emperor. During his reign Christian persecution was suspended and Christian worship was allowed by law. In what many consider a great compromise, there developed an accord, rather than an antagonistic relationship, between the Christian church and the imperial government. This led to the development of the just war theory.

This theory is based on a set of criteria used to determine if the use of force is justified. It was established in order to limit war and decrease violence: the idea was to make war the rare exception. Augustine's criteria said that the decision to go to war must be based on proving just cause, right intention, and legitimate authority. According to Augustine, merely the protection of private property or even self-defense of persons would not constitute a just reason for going to war. The criteria have become more nuanced over time, but just war criteria are still largely based on these three pillars, and they represent the majority view in most churches today.

In today's world, where there are civil wars, terrorist networks, nuclear weapons, and rogue states, the doctrine of just war is severely challenged. Many churches today claim that they support wars based on whether or not those wars meet the just war criteria. But how many people actually know what the criteria are?

Just war criteria are divided generally into two categories, designated by a pair of Latin phrases. The first, *jus ad bellum,* identifies the criteria that must be rigorously applied *before* going to war. The second, *jus in bello,* identifies the criteria for conducting oneself in the battlefield once one is already *in* a war.

The first set of criteria, applied before going to war, generally include the following:

1. *Just cause.* A just cause exists when war is necessary to protect innocents, to protect human rights, or to preserve conditions appropriate for human existence, but not for a narrowly defined national self-interest.
2. *Right intention.* Augustine argued that our love both for those attacked and for the attackers must be our driving motivation and that the only just goal is the restoration or establishment of a just peace.
3. *Legitimate authority.* Only recognized nations have the authority to declare and conduct wars. Under certain modern international agreements, even nation-states may not constitute legitimate authority.
4. *Reasonable likelihood of success.* Even if one is certain to "win the battle," one must be able to prove that there is a reasonable chance that use of force in the end will make the situation demonstrably better.
5. *Last resort.* Before military force is used, every other effort to resolve the injustice—including diplomacy and other nonviolent measures (such as third-party treaty inspections, embargoes or sanctions, and other forms of nonmilitary international pressure)—must be tried and given a reasonable chance of success.
6. *Comparative justice.* In just war criteria, the aggrieved party must have suffered an injustice substantially and measurably greater that what the other side has suffered.

According to just war theory, all of these criteria must be satisfied before one can allow for the use of military force, a quite rigorous test. The purpose is to steer legitimate authorities away from the use of force. Today, most (some would say all) contemporary wars fail to meet all the criteria.

Even in the waging of a war, it is not allowable for an authority to do "whatever it takes." Just war theory also maintains that a war must be *conducted* in a just fashion, using the following criteria:

1. *Discrimination.* The waging of war must discriminate between military and civilian targets, with no "intentional" targeting of the latter. For example, if you know that 15 percent of your "smart bombs" are going to miss their targets and if those targets are close to civilian facilities, can you really say the civilian deaths were "unintentional"?
2. *Proportionality.* The use of force must be proportional to the injustice that occurred, and the destruction and loss of life that will result from the use of force must be less than the anticipated good to be gained. Many, if not most, just war theorists would argue that this completely rules out the use—or threatened use—of nuclear, chemical, and biological weapons of any kind.
3. *Noncombatant immunity.* No one may intentionally attack those not directly engaged in the conflict—that is, civilians are immune. Some argue that any war that results in the loss of noncombatant lives is inherently unjust.
4. *Respect for the dignity of the enemy as a bearer of God's image.* It is wrong to demonize the enemy, especially as a method for garnering support for war. All combatants and prisoners should be treated with the dignity they deserve as human beings.
5. *Right intention.* The restoration of a just peace must be the primary focus in order to avoid the use of indiscriminate means and engaging in acts of revenge.

In the next section, we will consider the "war on terrorism," in general, and the war in Iraq, in particular. We will attempt to apply the just war criteria to each situation. In preparation, consider these questions:

1. The dictionary defines war as: (1) a state of usually open and declared armed hostile conflict between states or nations; (2) a period of such armed conflict; (3) a state of hostility, conflict, or antagonism; (4) a struggle or competition between opposing forces or for a particular end, such as a class war or a war against disease.[2] Under what definition would the "war on terrorism" come? Is the term applied metaphorically? Can you think of a better way to frame the issue?
2. Does the notion of a "preemptive" war fit the just war criteria? Why or why not?
3. Considering what you know about the war in Iraq, how does it conform to the criteria for a just war? In what ways does it not comply?

DAY 2

Considering the Evidence

Let's consider various aspects of the Iraq war in light of the just war criteria. First, review the criteria for going to war. These include just cause, right intention, legitimate authority, reasonable likelihood of success, last resort, and comparative justice.

Perhaps the easiest to consider is the criterion of *legitimate authority*. According to just war principles, as a nation-state the United States constitutes a legitimate authority. However, to the extent that the case for war was based on U.N. resolutions, the United States would not constitute a legitimate authority without U.N. approval. Furthermore, signatories to the U.N. Charter are not permitted to pursue war with other signatories unless they have U.N. approval. In the case of war against Iraq, under these conditions the United States is not the proper legitimate authority for pursuing war because (1) both the United States and Iraq are members of the United Nations, and (2) part of the case for war was based on U.N. resolutions. Therefore the United Nations would be the legitimate authority.

Did a *just cause* exist for the invasion of Iraq? The Bush administration's rationale for the war has varied over time, but the primary reasons cited have been these: (1) Iraq was allegedly involved with the terrorist attacks of September 11, 2001; (2) Iraq supposedly had weapons of mass destruction that threatened the United States; (3) Iraq stood in violation of U.N. resolutions; (4) Saddam Hussein was an evil leader who needed to be replaced.

The first two assertions, time has shown, were not true. The United States has not provided grounds for linking Iraq with the attacks of September 11. In fact, evidence shows that al Qaeda viewed Iraq as a secular Islamic state and therefore an enemy. Additionally, much of the "evidence" offered that Iraq had weapons of mass destruction was very thin and was contradicted by reports from inspection teams. In December 2005, President Bush finally admitted that, regarding Iraq's possession of weapons of mass destruction, "much of the intelligence turned out to be wrong."[3]

The third assertion, that Iraq was in violation of one or more U.N. resolutions, is indisputably true. But many observers believed the U.N. weapons inspections were successfully "containing" Iraq. In addition, other nations also stand in violation of U.N. resolutions. For example, Israel and Turkey have numerous violations, yet war has not been engaged against them. More important, however, is that the United Nations itself did not support war against Iraq as the best response to that country's clear violations.

Finally, Saddam Hussein was indeed a terrible dictator, but sadly there are many terrible dictators around the world. Military invasion and occupation of each of their countries is obviously not feasible, and such military intervention to effect "regime change"—which of course would violate international law—is not a just cause for war. Removing Saddam would be a just cause, but not by going to war with such costs and consequences.

Now let us examine the criterion of *right intention*. This is notoriously difficult to determine; most folks have enough trouble discerning their own motives. Right intention is to be judged on the basis of how a proposed war minimizes the "just cause"— the conditions that have led to a disturbance of the peace—and therefore restores peace. If there was no just cause for waging war on Iraq, then it is difficult to determine how one might assess right intention.

Was there a reasonable *likelihood of success* in launching war on Iraq? In other words, is it likely that the situation in Iraq will have improved after the war dramatically enough to outweigh the death and destruction resulting from the war? Notice that the standard is "likelihood," not "possibility." The history of Iraq, with its long-standing civil tensions, has to be taken into account. Border and boundary issues, along with deep ethnic divisions—which have not been resolved since Iraq was carved out of the Ottoman Empire by the French and British in 1920—must also factor into the "likelihood of success." U.S. military dominance was not in question as we contemplated war in Iraq. But was there reasonable likelihood that the United States could "win the peace"? The tragic events of the past three years have revealed major miscalculations.

Now, let's examine whether all other reasonable alternatives to war were tried before going to war. A very important issue is whether or not the sanctions and inspections imposed on Iraq were working. If inspections were working, then *last resort* had not been reached. As *God's Politics* notes, there was wide agreement among diverse Christian groups—and also among members of the United Nations—that the war was not necessary and that Iraq was being adequately "contained" by other means. The countries in the region surrounding Iraq did not agree that Saddam Hussein was an immediate threat. Finally, the evidence presented by the United States of Iraq's "imminent threat" in the run-up to the war was met with widespread skepticism. These skeptics have been proven right. By the criteria established, this was not a war of last resort.

To make the case for *comparative justice,* one would have to demonstrate that Hussein's rule in Iraq constituted a grave injustice against the United States—that the United States had suffered an injustice substantially and measurably greater than that suffered by the Iraqi people. An attempt to satisfy this criterion may have prompted the administration to try to link Iraq with the September 11 attacks, an allegation of connection that turned out to be false.

The overarching question we faced three years ago was, According to the six criteria, were the conditions surrounding the invasion of Iraq adequate for Christians to support the war as a just war? Most Christian bodies around the world concluded no.

Let's also consider the just war criteria that apply to how a war is conducted once it has begun. Since the war in Iraq is still under way, we do not have all the evidence, but we can examine these criteria based on what we currently know. The criteria include discrimination, proportionality, noncombatant immunity, right intention, and respect for the image of God in all humans.

U.S. forces use so-called smart munitions for "precision strikes" against urban populations in Iraq, targets that previously would have been off-limits because of the likelihood of civilian casualties. From 2003 to 2005, 53 percent of civilian deaths in Iraq involved explosive devices, with children disproportionately affected. "It appears that whatever their military advantages and benefit to soldiers," a dossier on Iraq war casualties states, "'stand-off' weapons which put a substantial distance between soldiers and their intended targets are the most likely to cause unintended harm to bystanders."[4] This alone is enough to challenge the criterion of *discrimination*.

The initial war strategy presented to the American public was a campaign of "shock and awe," a method of warfare intended to destroy the enemy's will to fight through an initial display of overwhelmingly destructive force. How should this be assessed in light of the criterion of *proportionality*?

Reports on civilian casualties during the war range from as low as 25,000 to more than 125,000. It appears that a significant percentage of those killed were noncombatants, mostly the elderly, women, and children. Given that, can we say that the United States has conducted this war in a fashion that satisfies the criterion of *noncombatant immunity*?

The criterion of *right intention* requires using only the force needed for the restoration of a just peace. Along with other aspects of the war, the cases of U.S. military personnel abusing and torturing prisoners—or allowing the conditions that led to the abuses—at Abu Ghraib and other detention centers constitute a failure to meet the requirements of right intention, as well as a violation of the final criterion, *respect for the dignity of the enemy* as a person bearing God's image. Wars are almost always characterized by the demonization of the other side, and we now have to factor in detainee abuse and prisoner torture as well.

So what is *your* assessment? From the perspective of just war criteria, is the U.S. war against Iraq just? Was it just to launch the war? Has it been conducted according to just war principles? And have these issues been adequately debated in the public discourse about the war?

Finally, can we apply the just war criteria to the so-called war on terrorism? To evaluate the conflict in light of the just war criteria, we would need to be able to talk about a war on specific terrorists, terrorist groups, and their supporters. From there, one could evaluate just cause, legitimate authority, right intention, last resort, etc.

Christians must engage critically with policies that are used to fight the war on terrorism. Even though terrorists always engage in activities that fail to meet the just war criteria (for example, targeting noncombatants), that does not guarantee that those fighting the terrorists are always acting justly. In other words, there may be injustice on both sides, and Christians ought to lead efforts aimed at redressing injustices that serve as a root cause of violence and that help to fuel terrorism.[5]

After September 11, most Americans wanted a strong response, and there were two paths that could have been taken. One spoke the language and spirit of justice and invoked the rule of law in promising to bring the perpetrators of terrorist violence to accountability. Those who so violated the standards of civilized life, and the human values we hold most dear, should never be allowed to escape judgment and punishment—and the danger of even more terror must be urgently prevented.

The other path used the language of war and invoked a spirit of retribution and even vengeance, emotions we can all understand. A "war on terrorism" summons up the strength and resolve to stop these horrific acts and prevent their cancerous spread. But the war language fails to provide moral and practical boundaries for that response. It often leads to indiscriminate retaliation and the "collateral damage" of even more loss of innocent life, as we have now seen in Iraq.

In the final analysis, a theory that simply analyzes whether a war is "just" is not enough—and throughout history, the just war theory has been used much more to justify war than to prevent it. Christians are called to go much deeper even than the prevention of war, to engage in pursuits that actively further the cause of peace.

Glen Stassen, a Christian ethicist at Fuller Theological Seminary in Pasadena, California, has identified ten practices involved in what he calls "just peacemaking." They include the following:

1. Support nonviolent direct action.
2. Take independent initiatives to reduce threat.
3. Use cooperative conflict resolution.
4. Acknowledge responsibility for conflict and injustice and seek repentance and forgiveness.
5. Advance democracy, human rights, and religious liberty.
6. Foster just and sustainable economic development.
7. Work with emerging cooperative forces in the international system.
8. Strengthen the United Nations and international efforts for cooperation and human rights.
9. Reduce offensive weapons and weapons trade.
10. Encourage grassroots peacemaking groups and voluntary associations.[6]

These practices could reduce both war and terrorism.

Perhaps one of the greatest challenges for Christians in the twenty-first century will be the development and strengthening of efforts like these, so that we can truly be about the things that make for peace.

DAY 3

Reading the Bible

Perhaps one of the most unfortunate aspects of much contemporary Bible reading is a tendency to see the Bible as a disparate collection of narratives and sayings, rather than a total work that must be taken in context. The Bible is a single story that moves from somewhere to somewhere. As the biblical literature unfolds, deeper movements become evident.

Let's examine several biblical passages relating to war, peace, and the use of violence. When those who support a given war are asked to provide a biblical basis, there is often an immediate appeal to the Hebrew scriptures (that is, the Old Testament). A person might say, "Well, God told Joshua to go to war against the inhabitants of the land. Therefore, God allows war." Passages such as the Joshua story in the Hebrew scriptures—texts that show God allowing war or explicitly commanding it—demonstrate, so the argument goes, God's toleration of war. Is this argument biblically sound? Or is this a proof-texting approach that ignores a larger movement within the Bible?

Vernard Eller, in *War and Peace: From Genesis to Revelation,* shows how the Bible's treatment of issues relating to the use of violence develops over time. Eller explains that, as the biblical story unfolds, God engages in acts and gives instruction to wean humans away from violence. Eller draws attention to the violence inherent in early societies. He points out how God's directions to people, though appearing harsh to us, were actually moves toward violence *reduction*. For example, the injunction to repay "an eye for an eye" was a move toward proportionality and away from clan wars that started as a result of a single death. To move humans away from violence, God calls a particular people who are to live in ways consistent with God's intentions.

In Deuteronomy 17, for example, God gives instructions that are aimed at keeping Israel reliant on God alone and—even when Israel has a king—forbidding them from putting their trust in military strength.

In the book of Isaiah, a major transition occurs in the biblical story arc as the image of the Suffering Servant is introduced. The new message from God is that redemptive violence is not the way to resist evil. Instead, redemptive suffering is the path God intends. In Isaiah 53, the Suffering Servant overcomes evil by taking on suffering rather than engaging in violent conflict. For Christians, the Suffering Servant foreshadows Jesus, but that imagery also stands as an indication of the norm God intends for human behavior.

By New Testament times—say, between the years 170 BCE and 140 CE—there was a belief within Judaism that the messiah would be a military leader who would reestablish a free homeland. It is noteworthy that Jesus never succumbed to pressure to join with the militant insurgent groups—called the Zealots—in an effort to oust the Romans from Jerusalem.

If we look directly into Jesus's own actions and teachings, we will find a clear portrayal of the nonviolent teacher of peace. For example, the Sermon on the Mount instructs us to be "peacemakers," to "turn the other cheek," and to "not resist evil with evil." Suffering and patience are indicated as praiseworthy. When Jesus is taken by the authorities and a disciple draws his sword in defense, Jesus instructs him to put the sword away. "All who take the sword," says Jesus, "will perish by the sword"

(Matthew 26:52). This warning against the use of violence is consistent with Jesus's teachings and actions throughout the gospels.

There are a few New Testament texts that are sometimes cited to claim that Jesus did not reject the use of violence. One is the "cleansing of the temple" (Matthew 21:12–13 and parallels). Some argue that Jesus used a whip to run the money-changers out of the temple. However, far from single-handedly overpowering the temple guard, it is more likely that Jesus used the whip to run the animals out of the temple. The fact that the whip used was one normally used to herd cattle only makes this a more likely reading. Another text cited is: "And let him who has no sword sell his mantle and buy one" (Luke 22:35–38). Why would Jesus tell someone to buy a sword, say those using this text in defense of violence, if he didn't intend for that person to use it? And yet we know that Jesus's intention was not to have weapons used to protect or defend him, because a few verses later he rebukes Peter for using the sword. In Luke 22:38, when Jesus is heading off to the Garden of Gethsemane, he indicates that they are going into a hostile situation. The disciples say that they have two swords, and Jesus responds, "It is enough." However, what he actually says is, "Enough!" Jesus is not affirming that they should bring along their swords. Rather, realizing that they have completely misunderstood his comment, he intends to cut off further discussion. "Stop, enough already!" is the intended message.

When these texts and images are taken together, one gets a powerful picture of God moving through time and teaching us that nonviolent suffering and even nonviolent resistance have primary place in the "battle" between good and evil. Jesus models this for us in his life and cross, and our call to be imitators of Christ means we must face this issue seriously. Can a person be both a Christian and a supporter of just war theory that allows the use of violence in extreme cases? Many have thought so—Augustine in the fourth century, Aquinas in the thirteenth, and others. In fact, today just war theory is more widely accepted than Christian pacifism.

So where do we go from there? Surely, there seems a strong preference for nonviolent resistance from the scriptural references we have seen. If we decide that this evidence can be overcome in a way that allows for just war, then we as Christians must certainly favor interpreting the criteria strictly.

DAY 4 — The Christian Tradition

Many Christians are surprised to learn that the early church overwhelmingly believed that to follow Jesus meant to reject the way of violence. Prior to 200 CE, most Christian voices argued against the participation of believers in war. From 200 CE to the Edict of Milan in 313 CE—when Constantine legalized Christianity—the vast majority of Christian teachers still taught and defended nonviolence as the only legitimate Christian option.

Consider the words, for example, of an early Christian theologian, Justin Martyr: "We who formerly murdered one another now refrain from making war even upon our enemies."[7] And, from Irenaeus, another early church leader, we hear similarly:

> The new covenant that brings back peace and the law that gives life have gone forth over the whole earth, as the prophets said: "For out of Zion will go forth the law, and the word of the Lord from Jerusalem; and the Lord will rebuke many people; and they will break down their swords into plowshares, and their spears into pruning hooks, and they will no longer learn to fight." ... These people [i.e., Christians] formed their swords and war-lances into plowshares ... that is, into instruments used for peaceful purposes. So now, they are unaccustomed to fighting. When they are struck, they offer also the other cheek.[8]

In both cases, the early church took Jesus's command to turn the other cheek and to pray for enemies as equivalent to commanding nonparticipation in war.

In several different places, Egyptian church teacher Clement of Alexandria also denied Christians the use of violence. Here are a couple of examples: "It is not in war, but in peace, that we are trained"; and "Christians are not allowed to use violence to correct the delinquencies of sins."[9]

Early Christian apologist Tertullian was even more direct, taking on the question of participation in war directly:

> "Nation will not take up sword against nation, and they will no more learn to fight." Who else, therefore, does this prophecy apply to, other than us? For we are fully taught by the new law, and therefore observe these practices.... The practice of the old law was to avenge itself by the vengeance of the sword. It was to pluck out "eye for eye," and to inflict retaliatory revenge for injury. However, the teaching of the new law points to clemency. It changes the primitive ferocity of swords and lances to tranquility. It remodels the primitive execution of war upon the rivals and enemies of the Law into the peaceful actions of plowing and cultivating the land.[10]

And again Tertullian wrote:

> A man cannot give his allegiance to two masters—God and Caesar.... How will a Christian man participate in war? In fact, how will he serve even in peace without a sword? For the Lord has taken the sword away. It is also true that soldiers came to John [the Baptist] and received the instructions for their conduct. It is true also that a centurion believed. Nevertheless, the Lord afterward, in disarming Peter, disarmed every soldier.[11]

Regarding someone who was already in the military when he become a Christian, Tertullian wrote, "[W]hen a man has become a believer and faith has been sealed, there must be either an immediate abandonment of the military office, which has been the course of many—or else all sorts of quibbling will have to be resorted to in order to avoid offending God."[12]

Roman church leader Hippolytus made a similar claim, writing: "A soldier of the civil authority must be taught not to kill men and to refuse to do so if he is commanded, and to refuse to take an oath. If he is unwilling to comply, he must be rejected for baptism.... If an applicant or a believer seeks to become a soldier, he must be rejected, for he has despised God."[13] During this period, there was little distinction between soldiers and the equivalent of police—the same force often served both functions. Some felt that Christians could participate in normal order-keeping exercises that police undertook. The problem came when the police officer was required to be a warrior and engage in killing.

Origen, another leader of the early church, wrote: "We have converted into pruning hooks the spears that were formerly used in war. For we no longer take up 'sword against nation,' nor do we 'learn war any more.' That is because we have become children of peace for the sake of Jesus, who is our Leader."[14]

The Christian position on war began to change when Constantine legalized Christianity with the Edict of Milan. The defense of the empire became increasingly intertwined with the protection of the church. By the time of Augustine (354–430 CE), the situation was ripe for his articulation of a Christian interpretation of the just war theory. Thus in a further compromise of its earlier view, the church moved from a position that completely rejected Christian participation in war to one that saw the use of force in the defense of the empire to be "wholly just." Since Augustine, the just war theory has undergone further refinement, as noted earlier, but most contemporary advocates of the just war theory appeal to his work.

The other main Christian position regarding war—pacifism or nonviolence—reemerged in the sixteenth-century Reformation with the Anabaptist tradition, and later in the Society of Friends. While a minority, these Christian traditions seek to be faithful to their understanding of the teachings of Jesus and the early church.

DAY 5 — Living Examples in the Contemporary Church

We often hear inspirational stories of great things done by individual persons. Often these stories do not tell us about the support community that was there to form, train, advise, and support those "individuals" who engage in heroic acts. Notice, in what follows, all the players involved in the formation of a young man named Shane. When he engaged in his acts for peace, he carried with him all those who had helped prepare him to act when the time came. The silent majority in the background is a powerful metaphor for the church.

LIVING FOR PEACE

Shane Claiborne was the popular kid in his high school. He was the prom king and part of the "in" crowd. He was planning on making it big, making lots of money, and living out his perception of the American dream. Shane also had a very typical faith experience for a kid in America. He made a faith decision at a Christian festival. He attended church. He became a part of a youth group—several of them, actually, attending whichever group had the most exciting offering at the time. So how, from this very traditional upbringing, did he end up in Iraq, at a time of war, promoting peace?

Well, there were a few steps in between.

Shane began to ask questions about why so many people who were following Jesus acted nothing like that man from Galilee. How did disciples become so unlike the One they claimed to be modeling their life after? Further, the life Christians were being called to lead seemed to have little to do with the great sacrifice that accompanied Jesus's life. Shane began to ask why "preachers were telling me to lay my life at the foot of the cross and weren't giving me anything to pick up."

Seeking to truly imitate Christ can have big consequences for an individual. Shane attended a Christian college (Eastern University), got involved with the poor and homeless in Philadelphia, and started a community of faith in the inner city in a place that had been abandoned by many within the church. Following Jesus can take you to crazy places. In Shane's case, it also ended up taking him to Iraq.

After the September 11 terrorist attacks, the whole nation wondered how to react. Nowhere was this discussion more active than in the U.S. churches. The world turned to America asking, "What would Jesus do?"

The initial response of the nation was patriotic. In the year following the attacks, the United States imported $51.7 million worth of American flags, most of which, ironically, were made in China. There was a great sense that the nation was united, and favorability ratings for public officials reached all-time highs.

In the two years after the attacks, the United States invaded Afghanistan, seeking the terrorists responsible for the September 11 attacks. By March 2003, sights were set on Iraq. Shane Claiborne saw the country as blindly rushing into an invasion for which we had no justification. Rather than simply joining the ranks of those content to complain about the illegal war on Iraq, Shane chose to act.

In the six months leading up to the invasion of Iraq, Shane fasted and prayed. He sought the direction of his Christian community. In the end, he knew that he was being called to Iraq to speak of God's peace. He joined the Iraq Peace Team, which consisted of priests and other clergy, veterans, doctors, journalists, and students. In the war zone, he hoped to offer the peaceful message of Jesus. (His war journals can be read online at www.thesimpleway.org/macro/shane_iraq.html.)

Shane went over to show others the love of Jesus and was amazed to find radical followers of Jesus already there. He went over to help transform the situation and was transformed himself. The popular kid, the prom king, was now the peace activist.

Shane's actions had an impact on people beyond those he met in Iraq. His war journals have been a great inspiration to others, as news of his actions spread virally on the Internet, and he has been invited to speak in significant places.

Inspired by stories like Shane's, a group of students at Asbury Seminary in Kentucky began gathering every Monday evening to pray for reconciliation in the world and to ask how it might begin in their own personal relationships. They are not ready to go to a foreign land and put themselves in the line of fire, but they are asking what part they could play in bringing peace to the world.

Shane would not consider what he has done exceptional. He would tell you that he was just following Jesus.

WILL SAMSON*

DAY 6 — Putting Faith into Action

The appropriate ways to live out "God's politics" with regard to war and peace will depend upon the contemporary situation in which we find ourselves. Do we live in a time or culture of peace? Are we merely "between wars"? Are we in the prewar buildup stage? Or the postwar cleanup? Or is our nation currently at war?

Let us consider the different phases along with the sorts of actions that might be appropriate to each. Of course, any of these actions can be undertaken during any of the phases.

During a period of relative peace, there are two important activities that need engagement. Begin by supporting organizations, causes, movements, or projects that are aimed at sowing the seeds of peace.[15] These might include victim-offender reconciliation projects, conflict resolution efforts in countries with a history of strife, racial and economic justice programs, or similar projects that dig deeply into bringing people together who are divided by difference or history and giving them the necessary tools to build a better future together. Choose one or two that you can actually participate in within your own community.

Many Christians are not knowledgeable enough about how the church has viewed war and peace. Classes can be organized to address the subject, and materials can be prepared that help deepen people's understanding of the issue. Bring in practitioners as well as educators so that the information is linked to real people living these issues today. Once the group has learned and discussed these traditions, consider bringing in representatives from other faith traditions (such as Judaism, Islam, and Hinduism) to discuss their faith's tradition regarding war and peace.

---

* *Will Samson is a student at Asbury Theological Seminary in Wilmore, Kentucky.*

When a nation is preparing for war, an adequate understanding of faith-based views on war becomes critical for persons to have rational, accurate, and critical participation in the public discourse. It is important for churches to help their members gather accurate information about the conflict, as well as to help them present a perspective rooted in the church's commitment to peacemaking. Then awareness can be translated into participation in the public discourse. Churches should be places of moral and ethical leadership for the whole community. This means providing the guiding principles of our Christian tradition and helping people apply them to the current situation. Letters to the editor, opinion pieces, letters to Congress and the administration, Web sites, and open forums should aim to instruct, educate, and give witness to our beliefs—not berate. Christians should state clearly and succinctly our position on the war and the theological or ethical principles that led us to that conclusion. It might be appropriate to undertake public demonstrations, prayer vigils, or other nonviolent actions to demonstrate the urgency of the situation. In all these actions, it is important to come to collective discernment and understanding within a spiritual community or community of faith.

If war breaks out, then many of the steps indicated in the preceding paragraph may still be in order, though now it becomes critical to intensify those activities. At some point, acts of civil disobedience might also be appropriate. This is a serious step that should be undertaken only by those who have been through nonviolence training, and only at the end of an extended period of negotiation with those in positions of power who are making the decisions about war. Once war breaks out, lives will be lost on both sides. Unfortunately, noncombatants will likely suffer most. This realization only makes more evident the critical nature of our participation. Review in some detail the activities proposed in the appendix, and look for more creative ways to reduce violence and teach people how to resist the temptation to use violence to resolve conflicts.

DAY 7 — Group Meeting and Reflection

1. An alternative response to the terrorist attacks on September 11 is outlined on page 91 of *God's Politics*. Assume a major newspaper came to you and asked that you provide a plan that offered an appropriate religious response to September 11. What would your points be? Why did you choose them?

2. Serious attempts to undermine terrorism must include a willingness on the part of the powerful to examine their own past mistakes and genuinely attempt to rectify them. Research what some of those mistakes might be. What things come to mind?

3. Discuss "Ten Lessons to Defeat Terrorism" (*God's Politics*, page 105). Identify strengths and weaknesses. What would you add?

4. Discuss and assess "Lessons of War" (*God's Politics*, page 120).

5. Reflect upon "Putting Down the Mighty from Their Thrones" (*God's Politics*, page 129). How would you characterize the reversal of power relations described there? To what extent do the gospels, in fact, reverse these relations? What does it mean to live out this reversal in our everyday lives?

6. *God's Politics* quotes columnist George Will's comments on domination (page 146). Discuss the quote and assess it from a theological perspective.

7. Discuss preemptive peacemaking strategies—that is, methods and engagements that might be undertaken prior to the outbreak of war that would advance a just peace. You might begin by identifying issues that would constitute an injustice that could lead to war.

8. *God's Politics* cites Gerald Schlabach's work (page 165), drawing attention to the differences between how police forces operate and how militaries operate. How might these concepts be brought to bear at an international level to avoid war?

9. To what extent do you think the Israeli-Palestinian conflict drives international terrorism? What steps would you support to bring about a just peace in the Middle East?

10. Chapter 12 of *God's Politics* has the subtitle "Cure Causes, Not Just Symptoms." What are some of the underlying causes of global insecurity? What contribution do we make to those causes? How might we contribute instead to global security—both in our personal lives and choices and in our participation as citizens who influence national policies?

Economic Justice

GOD'S POLITICS asks what it means for an economy to be structured in a way that constitutes justice for all of its members. There are implicit advantages and disadvantages for different participants in free economies. We have to consider what factors, from a Christian perspective, must guide our arguments for reforming economic practices and institutions. This theme relates particularly to chapters 12, 13, 16, and 17 in *God's Politics*. Read or review those chapters. Below is a brief recap.

Chapter 12: The chapter begins by recognizing the role fear plays in how we respond to threats and the extent to which we feel vulnerable. It ends with the recognition that lasting peace must be based on a sense of security that includes personal, national, and global levels. Real security means, among other things, the assurance that all people have access to the essentials of life—such as adequate food, water, and housing. The prophet Micah offers a vision of the world where swords are beaten into plowshares and where nations do not make war against other nations. He goes on to envision everyone having their own "vine and fig tree," living free and unafraid. Bringing about a secure future and making that vision a reality will require dealing with causes and not merely symptoms.

Chapter 13: Thousands of Bible verses affirm our obligation to care for the poor. Despite this clear and abundant teaching, some people try to argue that when Jesus said, "The poor you will have always with you" (Matthew 26:11), it somehow provided justification for doing little or nothing about poverty—as if Jesus had said there would always be poor people among us, so why do anything about it? However, this misreads both the immediate and the broader contexts of his words. First, this verse comes after Jesus's anointing by the woman at Bethany, prior to his death on the cross—Jesus will not be among the disciples for much longer: "You will not always have me." Second, Jesus is making a judgment about the social location of his followers—that to follow Jesus means we will always have the opportunity, and the gift, of working on behalf of those he called "the least of these."

Chapter 16: Former Treasury Secretary Paul O'Neill said, "Part of the genius of capitalism [is that] people get to make good decisions or bad decisions. And they get to pay the consequences or enjoy the fruits of their decisions."[1] Yet corporate traders and executives who make really bad decisions rarely "pay the consequences."

More often it is the workers and consumers who suffer the results. When self-interest and profit are placed ahead of the common good, those most vulnerable suffer the most. In the longer term, we all suffer the subsequent breakdown in society. The Bible includes specific commands intended to prevent the accumulation of extreme wealth, because this is directly tied to abuse of the poor.

Chapter 17: There seems to be a new level of interest in addressing global poverty. At the same time, however, the global community has fallen behind in its efforts to meet the U.N.'s Millennium Development Goals (which we'll look at on Day 2) in the crucial areas of education, health, and targeted poverty reduction. For the first time in history, we have the information, knowledge, technology, and resources to bring the worst of global poverty to an end. What we seem to be lacking is the moral and political will to do so. Taking advantage of poor countries is too easy for developed nations and multinational corporations that are eager to increase profits. People of faith need to lead the way in generating new moral energy for addressing global poverty.

DAY 1 — Introducing the Topic

Before we can begin a discussion of economic justice, we must spend some time working through definitions of the term—what exactly is *economic justice*? Obviously, to use the term "economic" is to speak of buying, selling, and trading various goods and services, but what would make one way of "doing economy" more or less "just" than another? This requires a definition of justice, and for followers of Jesus it must be one that is consistent with the Bible and Christian teaching.

Plato and Aristotle defined justice as giving to a person what that person deserves. Unfortunately, this led Plato to distinguish between persons based upon their "quality" or "virtue." Thus a person wasn't measured by individual acts or choices, but by his or her place in society as ruler, soldier, or "other." This led to certain rules of justice being seen as appropriate for certain kinds of people: certain laws applied to the ruling class, while another set of rules applied to laborers or slaves. Justice did not mean that all received equal opportunity.

Justice more consistent with Christian teaching reflects the very character and intentions of God. And since all human beings possess the equality of being created in God's image, it means equal opportunities, regardless of race, class, gender, or other discriminatory factors. It necessarily includes aspects of divine mercy, since God's actions are both just and merciful. We cannot drive a wedge between the notions of justice and mercy. This invites us, as Christians, to see God's own actions as embodying perfect justice, while also embodying mercy.

Similarly, while we must affirm "equality" in some sense in our affirmation of justice, we do not have to conceive of justice as dictating "equality" of outcomes.

In other words, a just economic playing field does not require that all persons have the exact same income, live in the same size house, etc. In fact, rewards for various types of work may vary, as long as the variations are not disproportionate to the quality and quantity of work. However, this is no carte blanche to make the moral standard "what the market will bear," because history frequently shows that the market operates unjustly.

The American Friends Service Committee summarizes principles that promote a just economic playing field as follows:

> Economic justice means building a fair economy that works for everyone. It means fair trade policies that protect workers' rights to organize and to receive a living wage for their work at home and abroad. It includes budget and tax policies in which corporations and wealthy individuals pay their fair share, and which support good schools and childcare, affordable healthcare and housing, retirement security, and a safety net for those in need. It promotes the common good by funding public services. It means calling for new national priorities that reduce wasteful military spending and redirect tax dollars to helping our children, elders, and communities meet their needs. It includes notions of a social contract in which society and individuals fulfill their mutual responsibilities to each other.[2]

The National Association of Evangelicals puts it this way:

> Economic justice includes both the mitigation of suffering and also the restoration of wholeness. Wholeness includes full participation in the life of the community. Health care, nutrition, and education are important ingredients in helping people transcend the stigma and agony of poverty and re-enter community. Since healthy family systems are important for nurturing healthy individuals and overcoming poverty, public policy should encourage marriage and sexual abstinence outside marriage, while discouraging early onset of sexual activity, out-of-wedlock births, and easy divorce. Government should also hold fathers and mothers responsible for the maintenance of their families, enforcing where necessary the collection of child-support payments. Restoring people to wholeness means that governmental social welfare must aim to provide opportunity and restore people to self-sufficiency. While basic standards of support must be put in place to provide for those who cannot care for their families and themselves, incentives and training in marketable skills must be part of any well-rounded program. We urge Christians who work in the political realm to shape wise laws pertaining to the creation of wealth, wages, education, taxation, immigration, health care, and social welfare that will protect those trapped in poverty and empower the poor to improve their circumstances.[3]

These summaries begin to get at the issues that connect the terms "justice" and "economy." For a deeper and more thorough examination, we could hardly do better than to cite the ten principles drawn from the U.S. Catholic bishops' 1986 pastoral letter on Catholic social teaching and the U.S. economy, titled *Economic Justice for All*. The ten principles are listed below.

1. The economy exists for the person, not the person for the economy.
2. All economic life should be shaped by moral principles. Economic choices and institutions must be judged by how they protect or undermine the life and dignity of the human person, support the family, and serve the common good.
3. A fundamental moral measure of any economy is how the poor and vulnerable are faring.
4. All people have a right to life and to secure the basic necessities of life (e.g., food, clothing, shelter, education, health care, safe environment, economic security).
5. All people have the right to economic initiative, to productive work, to just wages and benefits, to decent working conditions, as well as to organize and join unions and other associations.
6. All people, to the extent they are able, have a corresponding duty to work, a responsibility to provide for the needs of their families, and an obligation to contribute to the broader society.
7. In economic life, free markets have both clear advantages and limits; government has essential responsibilities and limits; voluntary groups have irreplaceable roles, but cannot substitute for the proper working of the market and the just policies of the state.
8. Society has a moral obligation, including governmental action where necessary, to assure opportunity, meet basic human needs, and pursue justice in economic life.
9. Workers, owners, managers, stockholders, and consumers are moral agents in economic life. By our choices, initiative, creativity, and investment, we enhance or diminish economic opportunity, community life, and social justice.
10. The global economy has moral dimensions and human consequences. Decisions on investment, trade, aid, and development should protect human life and promote human rights, especially for those most in need wherever they might live on this globe.

In addition, in his 1991 encyclical *Centesimus Annus*, Pope John Paul II noted that Christian faith envisions a "society of work, enterprise, and participation" that "is not directed against the market, but demands that the market be appropriately controlled by the forces of society and by the state to assure that the basic needs of the whole society are satisfied."[4] In the midst of our responsibilities, we must hear the call to devote particular attention to those on the margins of society, who are particularly exposed to life's uncertainties.

Economic justice, then, is not merely about equality, nor is it something that one can easily profile on a chart, reduce to numbers, or bring about via hard and fast rules. Rather, to engage in the struggle for economic justice is to recognize that we must learn to understand circumstances through an integration of God's justice, mercy, grace, and love. Our first engagement must be driven by the call to love God by loving our neighbors as ourselves.

Two things, then, are at the center of economic justice: (1) recognition that God expects each of us to engage in acts of mercy and justice aimed at creating a fair and just economic playing field, and (2) recognition that God intends that public institutions have their own role to play in establishing just economies. Pope John Paul II summarized these factors in noting that Christians are not opposed to the free market but demand that it be policed in order to serve the common good.[5]

DAY 2

Considering the Evidence

Given this understanding of economic justice, particularly as summarized in the ten principles named by the Catholic bishops, it is pretty clear that both domestically and internationally the United States faces a number of challenges. In what ways can we work to develop economic systems that better embody those principles? Again, from the American Friends Service Committee:

> In today's global economy, many people are experiencing hunger, hardship, and the impact of a growing inequality of wealth, power, and access to basic resources. Around the world, 1.2 billion people live in "extreme" poverty. Here at home, 45 million Americans lack health insurance, and 1 in 3 cannot afford decent housing. Meanwhile, more than 60 percent of U.S. corporations paid no federal taxes for 1996 through 2000. The total net worth of America's 3,000 wealthiest individuals reached $955 billion while the median weekly wage for an American worker was $625.[6]

How can we accept that some live in extreme poverty and lack access to basic health care while some live with extreme wealth and the most profitable corporations go tax-free? Many of those who live in extreme poverty try to survive on the equivalent of $1 per day while the richest 3,000 persons hold wealth of nearly $1 trillion. Can we consider any economic system just that creates and allows such inequities to exist? Unfortunately, the story gets worse.

As chapter 17 of *God's Politics* notes, in September 2000 the United Nations established an agenda for overcoming fundamental economic injustices on a global level. The development targets were called the Millennium Development

Goals (MDGs). They outlined poverty reduction goals to be accomplished by the year 2015. Eight goals covered the eradication of extreme poverty, primary school education for all children, gender equality, reduction of infant mortality rates, improved health care for mothers, environmental care, and international cooperation for global development. In September 2005, the U.N.'s annual Human Development Report concluded that little progress had been made on these goals and that fifty countries had actually lost ground on at least one of them. The report noted growing disparities of wealth and poverty both within and between countries as well as disparate access to resources and distribution of power. Let's look at some specifics.

- According to current trends, 827 million people will live in extreme poverty in 2015.
- Fifty countries are currently falling behind target on at least one Millennium Development Goal.
- A further sixty-five countries risk failing to reach at least one of the goals by the year 2040.
- In eighteen countries, the current Human Development Index (HDI: a measure of poverty, literacy, education, and life expectancy for countries worldwide) is lower than it was in 1990, when the index was first produced. Twelve of these countries are in Africa, and the other six are former Soviet republics.
- The twenty-four countries with the lowest HDI rating are all in Africa, with Niger at the very bottom of the list.
- The fifty persons in the world with the most personal wealth have combined income that exceeds that of the poorest 416 million.
- There are 2.5 billion people (40 percent of the world's population) currently living on less than $2 per day.
- These 2.5 billion are the recipients of only 5 percent of the world's income, while the richest 10 percent receive 54 percent of the global income.
- The gap between the richest and poorest is growing in 80 percent of these countries while it is declining in only 4 percent.[7]

These facts paint a picture of global inequity and a corresponding increase in those suffering at the lowest end of the income strata. The U.N.'s 2005 Human Development Report notes that while "some important human development advances have been registered ... the overall report card on progress makes for depressing reading." The report goes on to identify the implementation of policies aimed to reduce income and wealth distribution inequities as the highest priority.

Many rightly put attention on trade issues as central to establishing a just global economy. As the U.N. report notes, "Trade policies of rich countries generally greatly disadvantage developing countries." For example, since rich countries have disproportionate representation in trade-negotiating processes, they are able to further slant the playing field in their favor, and generally do so.

The International Monetary Fund (IMF) is an international organization created by the United Nations in 1946 as part of a financial reconstruction effort in the wake of World War II. It was created to oversee the global finance system by monitoring exchange rates and balance of payments as well as providing loans to countries and monitoring repayments. The IMF regularly requires countries borrowing from the fund to accept certain "conditionals" before they can receive funds. These conditionals require the borrower to privatize public institutions and to open their markets to free trade, with little concern for the damage done to low-income people.

Further, while rich countries typically require that developing countries open their own markets to free trade, those rich countries often continue protectionist policies for their own markets, such as farm subsidies to protect their farmers against lower-cost producers in other countries. The United Nations estimates that this practice alone costs developing economies $72 billion per year. Given that the United Nations has estimated that the entire world's hungry could be fed for $40 billion per year, these agricultural subsidies are literally starving people in developing countries.

If we turn our attention back to the United States, we will also find some very disturbing numbers. In order to get a glimpse into the seriousness of the gap between the rich and the poor, we have to look at both the wealth gap and the income gap. In 2001, it was estimated that the total net worth of Americans was $42.4 trillion. The "wealth" pie was divided up as follows:

- The richest 1 percent held 32.7 percent of all wealth.
- The richest 5 percent held 57.7 percent of all wealth.
- The richest 10 percent held 69.7 percent of all wealth.
- The richest 50 percent held 97.2 percent of all wealth.
- The poorest 50 percent held 2.8 percent of all wealth.[8]

The wealth gap has been growing for some time. For example, from 1983 to 1998, the richest 1 percent of Americans saw their share of wealth increase by 42.2 percent while the poorest 40 percent saw their share of wealth decline by more than 76 percent.

Income distribution in 2001 was not quite as severely skewed as wealth distribution, but it was still quite one-sided. Here's a look at the "income" pie:

- The top 5 percent had 21 percent of all income.
- The top 20 percent had 47.7 percent of all income.
- The top 40 percent had 70.6 percent of all income.
- The top 60 percent had 86 percent of all income.
- The lowest 20 percent only had 4.2 percent of all income.
- The lowest 40 percent only had 14 percent of all income.[9]

Of course, it is understandable that wealth distribution would diverge even more than income distribution. Those on the low end of the income scale are expending most or all of their income to purchase life's necessities, while those on the high end are investing most of theirs and thus increasing their wealth. Over time, this accumulation of wealth in the hands of a few also gathers political and market power in their hands. This slants the playing field ever steeper to the advantage of the rich.

DAY 3 — Reading the Bible

What does the Bible have to say about economic justice, which is closely related to the concept of mutual responsibility? According to scripture, does God intend for us primarily to "watch out for number one," or are we called to give ourselves for each other in relationships of deep interdependence?

Many passages throughout the Bible are best understood within this context, and several early ones are of particular importance. The early chapters of Genesis give an accounting of God's creation of the world, the subsequent disobedience of humans, and the various consequences that led to a world spiraling ever deeper into chaos. In Genesis 12, we find the beginning of God's plan to set things right with the call of Abraham. Notice in particular that, in verse 3, Abraham is being called not just to be blessed *but in order that he might be a blessing to all*. Similar language is picked up when Abraham is told that he will be a blessing to the other nations. Already we see an important aspect of the deeply interdependent nature of the lives that God intends for us.

Then we come to the fifteenth chapter of Deuteronomy. The idea of being called to serve God for the sake of others is expressed in several ways in this chapter. First, God indicates that there will be no one in need because God will provide adequately. But God also gives instructions on how to structure a "Sabbath economy" based on certain social disciplines. These included gleaning laws (that is, laws requiring that some fruit be left in the fields for the poor) and clearing the slate for those in debt bondage every seventh year. "Such legislated social disciplines of wealth restructuring in Israel were intended as a hedge against the tendency of human societies to concentrate power and wealth in the hands of the few, creating hierarchical classes with the poor at the bottom," writes theologian Ched Myers. "The vision was that if 'Sabbath economics' was practiced," Myers continues, "then 'There will be no one in need among you' (Deuteronomy 15:4). But the practical Deuteronomist, anticipating rightly that the people would forever be hedging on the demands of social justice, adds that compassion is the plumb line of the law: 'For there will never cease to be needy ones in your land, I command you: Open your hand to the poor' (Deuteronomy 15:11)."[10]

In this brief picture of an economy consistent with God's intentions, God gives primary attention to mechanisms intended to prevent the rise of a class of permanently dispossessed people and a class of those with extreme wealth. Sounds a lot like a system built on the concern for economic justice, doesn't it?

Leviticus 25 also addresses a periodic leveling of the economic playing field through "years of jubilee." Every fiftieth year, all lands were to be returned to their ancestral owners—again, a specific means to prevent vast accumulations of wealth in the hands of a few. This likewise would keep people from hedging on the social justice that God requires.

Another example of God's concern for the poor and desire for a just economic system is expressed in the laws about collateral. "If ever you take your neighbor's garment in pledge, you shall restore it to him before the sun goes down; for that is his only covering and it is his mantle for his body; in what else shall he sleep?" (Exodus 22:26–27, RSV). God's sense of economic justice is precisely the reverse of our own economic practices. When a poor, "higher-risk" person wants to borrow from a bank, higher fees and interest are demanded, or loans are simply denied. God, however, is more interested in the care of the poor.

The prophet Amos also reveals the intensity of God's concern for basic economic justice:

> Thus says the Lord: For three transgressions of Israel, and for four, I will not revoke the punishment; because they sell the righteous for silver, and the needy for a pair of sandals—they who trample the head of the poor into the dust of the earth, and push the afflicted out of the way; father and son go in to the same girl, so that my holy name is profaned; they lay themselves down beside every altar on garments taken in pledge; and in the house of their God they drink wine bought with fines they imposed. (Amos 2:6–9)

Here God pronounces judgment on the nation of Israel because of its failures to act with economic justice. First, Israel has become a nation that sells the poor so that those in power may accumulate more wealth. Second, the failure to observe God's commands to care for the poor and marginalized has led other nations to blaspheme God's name. How so? When by not living up to God's intentions we call into question both God's goodness and God's very existence, our sin leads others to make faulty judgments about God. Third, the reference to "garments taken in pledge" announces perverse disobedience of God's command that those garments are to be returned by sunset. Not only are they kept, but now the holders are using them for their own luxury before the very altar of God!

Since God has given these instructions as part of the laws of Israel, it is impossible to claim that God intends care for the poor to occur only in the "private sphere." In these and other passages, God gives commands to the people corporately and punishes them corporately for their failure to obey.

Since public institutions play a major role in the shape of our shared lives, it would not be possible to order our lives in a way that is consistent with God's intentions without involving these public institutions. Any serious attempt to live in a way that is consistent with God's expectations cannot exclude a role for governments and other social institutions.

This point is amplified in Ezekiel 16. God is again about to pronounce judgment on Israel. This time God compares the Israelites' sins to the sins of the citizens of Sodom. According to Ezekiel 16: "This was the guilt of your sister Sodom: She and her daughters had pride, excess of food, and prosperous ease, but did not aid the poor and needy. They were haughty, and did abominable things before me; therefore I removed them when I saw it" (verses 49–50). Tony Campolo, emeritus professor at Eastern University, once noted that if the sins of Sodom constituted "sodomy," then sodomy includes pride, luxury, and the failure to hear the cry of the needy. Again, economic justice is front and center.

Next let's consider Jesus's own teachings. His warnings about economic justice show up regularly. Unfortunately, perhaps because many read them from a social position of affluence, these passages are often muted in interpretation or preaching. For example, how often do we think deeply about God's judgment on the man whose crops were so plentiful that he planned to tear down his barns and build bigger ones? What's wrong with that? He earned it all through hard work—why not retire early? However, when this man took the bounty of God as his own personal property, God called him a fool. Of course, this does not come as a surprise once we reflect upon the intimate connections between Jesus's mission statement in Luke 4 and the issues we've already examined from the Hebrew scriptures. Consider Luke 4:18–19:

> The Spirit of the Lord is upon me, because he has anointed me to bring
> good news to the poor. He has sent me to proclaim release to the captives
> and recovery of sight to the blind, to let the oppressed go free, to proclaim
> the year of the Lord's favor.

The immediate context advises us that Jesus is quoting from the prophet Isaiah, and many have pointed out the "Jubilee-like" language repeated here. While Jesus is not limiting his ministry to what we would call economic or social justice issues, he clearly adopts them as a central part of his ministry and mission in the world. For example, in the account of the final judgment in Matthew 25, care for "the least of these" moves front and center and becomes the basis by which to identify those who are or are not Jesus's followers.

Consider the story of the rich man and Lazarus in Luke 16:19–31. Lazarus, as far as we know, is not a relative of the rich man, nor does Lazarus have any claim on the rich man other than being a fellow human in need. We know that the rich man "dressed in purple and the finest linen and feasted in great magnificence every day" (verse 19). Lazarus is "full of sores, and desiring to be fed with the crumbs which fell from the rich man's table" (20). Note the extreme wealth gap. God takes very seriously that the rich man does not expend any of his great wealth to ease Lazarus's suffering. The rich man's neglect to care for Lazarus is the most significant factor in determining the rich man's fate—namely, that he goes to hell!

Concern for the poor and others on the margins of society also appears in the epistles of the early church. For example, the letter of James covers the threat of greed and materialism from a number of perspectives. The writer reminds us that riches and material goods are transitory, hardly worth as much energy as we normally invest in them (see James 1:9–11). If we are to imitate Jesus, we can't treat other people differently according to their wealth status. God is not a respecter of wealth, nor should we be (see James 2:1–13). Finally, the writer strongly admonishes that wealth obliges us not only to pray for the poor, but also to assist them (James 2:14–17).

Paul, in 2 Corinthians 8:15, describes the economy of the first Christians by drawing on the book of Exodus when he writes that "the one who had much did not have too much, and the one who had little did not have too little." Here, Paul suggests that we should be aware of the needs around us and use any extra we might have to help meet them. This challenges the contemporary tendency to allow ourselves to be driven only by self-interest.

We could easily extend our study into many, many other places within scripture, but we will leave that as an exercise to the reader. What is clear is that God takes economic justice seriously, at the level of the individual person, at the level of the church, and at the level of public institutions.[11]

DAY 4

The Christian Tradition

The biblical test of any economic structure is whether we count the interests of others as being as important as our own, and how well we protect the poor. Did the early church pick up on these concerns from scripture? Yes, they did.

In the twenty-first century, there has been a strong tendency to view economics from a mostly capitalist, free-market perspective. Because of this, some of the early church's teachings may sound strange to us.

The early church had mixed feelings with regard to private property. Generally it was affirmed, but with the recognition that all that one "owns" is really held under stewardship from God. Given that, the church emphasized the obligation to steward one's resources in a way that aimed to meet the needs of others. Jesuit writer William Ryan notes that "in the 17th century we find Bossuet, the renowned preacher at Notre Dame Cathedral in Paris, telling the rich that they must care for the poor, for it is only they [the poor] who can open the gates of heaven for the rich."[12]

The question of what constituted a fair profit was another subject that both the early church leaders and later Christians addressed. The concern for justice was always at the forefront. Justice was understood not as "what the market would bear," but rather as what served human need and community. For example, Thomas Aquinas, writing in the thirteenth century, argued: "To keep back what is due another"—such as a fair wage—"inflicts the same kind of injury as taking a thing unjustly."[13]

On the communal nature of the world's resources and our obligation to use them to benefit the common good, hear Ambrose of Milan, a fourth-century bishop:

> Why do the injuries of nature delight you? The world has been created for all, while you rich are trying to keep it for yourselves. Not merely the possession of the earth, but the very sky, air and the sea are claimed for the use of the rich few.... Not from your own do you bestow on the poor man, but you make return from what is his. For what has been given as common for the use of all, you appropriate for yourself alone. The earth belongs to all, not to the rich.[14]

Again, in our contemporary setting, ownership and utilization of the earth's resources are often seen very differently than they were by the Christians who lived closest to the time of Jesus. For example, how many of these warnings offered by Ambrose could be connected directly to legislation passed within the last few years that radically individualizes the ownership of natural resources, cutting the connection to a broader community?

We've already mentioned the story of Lazarus and the rich man from the second half of Luke 16, but how many have ever heard it preached like this?

> Indeed Lazarus suffered no injustice from the rich man; for the rich man did not take Lazarus' money, but failed to share his own. If he is accused by the man he failed to pity because he did not share his own wealth, what pardon will the man receive who has stolen others' goods, when he is surrounded by those whom he has wronged? I shall bring you testimony from divine Scripture, saying that not only the theft of others' goods but also the failure to share one's own goods with others is theft and swindle and defraudation.
>
> ... [Y]ou have stolen the goods of the poor. [The] rich hold the goods of the poor even if they have inherited them from their fathers or no matter how they have gathered their wealth. Deprive not the poor of his living. To deprive is to take what belongs to another; for it is called deprivation when we take and keep what belongs to others. By this we are taught that when we do not show mercy, we shall be punished just like those who steal. For money is the Lord's, however we may have gathered it.[15]

St. John Chrysostom, who wrote the above, might not last long in today's churches if he so boldly charged the rich with their obligations to the poor!

The wealth that comes our way comes with obligations and accountabilities, as do all things that one holds in trust. Our economic life must be driven by a love and concern for the poor among us and around the world. The idea that economic justice could bear any resemblance to social Darwinism ("survival of the most economically fit") would have been foreign, even repugnant, to the early church.

DAY 5

Living Examples in the Contemporary Church

Advocacy for greater economic justice often seems futile. What can one person or a small group of people really do? The following story about how two women in a local church affected the views of their member of Congress on debt relief suggests that one person *can* make a difference.

JUBILEE BEGINS WITH ME

Pat Pelham lives in Birmingham, Alabama. About four years ago, she felt called to help people in need. Her pastor at Independent Presbyterian Church suggested she get their church involved in Bread for the World.

Pat and her friend Elaine Van Cleave came to hear me talk about Bread for the World at Our Lady of Sorrows Catholic Church. After that event, Pat and Elaine started to organize. They got their church's hunger committee involved in Bread for the World.

Three years ago, they invited their member of Congress, Rep. Spencer Bachus, to a Bread for the World dinner at Independent Presbyterian. I sat on his left, and the Presbyterian Hunger Action Enabler for Birmingham—a Republican Party activist—sat on his right. We urged Bachus to cosponsor the anti-hunger legislation that Bread for the World was pushing that year. Rep. Bachus had never before sponsored such legislation. But he called Pat the next evening and said, "I doubt that this will win me many votes, but I don't want to be responsible for even one child going hungry."

At the beginning of 1999, the Jubilee 2000 network was getting organized. Rep. Bachus had become chair of the international committee of the House Banking Committee, where any congressional action on debt relief would have to start. Pat, Elaine, and two friends from Independent Presbyterian flew up to Washington, D.C., at their own expense to take Bachus a debt-relief petition with 400 signatures.

"I don't know much about economics or international finance," Elaine explained. "But I do know that about 30,000 children die every day from hunger and other preventable causes, and, as a mother, that really bothers me. . . . [I]t would help a lot if you would sponsor this Jubilee legislation."

"What's the connection between so many children dying of hunger and debt relief?" Bachus asked. "All I know," Elaine said, "is that if I had to choose between paying a debt that I had inherited from my parents and buying food for my children, the choice would be clear." Bachus agreed to be an original sponsor of our bill and became its most passionate advocate.

Treasury Secretary Lawrence Summers told me that testifying before Bachus's subcommittee convinced him to change U.S. policy toward poor-country debt. If this conservative Republican urged cancellation of debts for the poorest countries, it was time for a change.

Spencer Bachus, a Southern Baptist, is a straightforward Christian. When the Banking Committee held its hearing on poor-country debt, Bachus said, "If we don't write off some of this debt, poor people in these countries will be suffering for the rest of their lives. And we'll be suffering a lot longer than that."

He held up a statement from Pope John Paul II and said, "I haven't read much by Catholics before, but I don't know how any Christian could read what the pope is saying here and not agree that we need to do something about the debt of these countries."

Bachus lobbied his conservative colleagues, including the Republican leadership of the House, for U.S. participation in international debt relief. Bachus says that he had come to see the world differently because of the church people back home who had approached him about Jubilee.

"I really hadn't thought much about places like Africa before," Bachus said. "Now, when Congress debates whether U.S. health care is too expensive at $2,200 per capita per year, I'm struck that a country like Ethiopia spends $10 on health care per capita per year."

Pat Pelham didn't do this by herself, of course, even in Birmingham. Across the country, several thousand people have been just as active as Pat on the Jubilee legislation. But there is a very clear line of causation between the grassroots activism of Pat and her friends in Birmingham and a significant breakthrough for justice in the world.

DAVID BECKMANN*

Ultimately, churches must get involved in building a more just economy at a variety of levels, all the way from encouraging individual giving to advocacy for appropriate public policies. Our witness is always stronger when we endeavor to put into practice in our local communities what we are defending more broadly. It is encouraging to find followers of Jesus who are putting into action the call to care for people living in poverty. Undoubtedly, there are many, many churches across our country that are seeking creatively to live out the divine call in our lives. We often hear a great deal about what is discouraging about the church today. Keep on the lookout, though, for these pearls of the kingdom of God.

DAY 6 — Putting Faith into Action

An important first step for engaging in activities intended to enhance economic justice is education. It is important to open a conversation that reveals the

---

* David Beckmann is president of Bread for the World. This text appeared in Sojourners, July/Aug. 2000, vol. 29, no. 4, p. 47.

basic inequities that exist. For example, why do some of the hardest workers end up with the lowest wages? Is it just for someone to work full-time and yet not make enough to care for her family? Is health care a luxury or a basic human right? What are the federal poverty guidelines for this year? How do these poverty markers compare to what it actually takes to live in the different parts of the country? What is the living wage movement all about, and how should Christians be involved with it?

There are two factors to keep in mind when working on education about economics. First, some of our most deeply seated presuppositions are held with regard to what constitutes economic fairness. It is important to include material from a range of sources in any educational program. This gives those from varying backgrounds and experiences several windows into the conversation. We need to give much attention to the biblical and theological justifications for economic justice concerns and how to address them. Second, this is an area that calls for creativity, such as dramatic or visual presentations of economic disparities that allow participants to see the consequences of economic injustice firsthand.

Once the education phase is completed, there are numerous ways to become involved in the ongoing debate. Write letters to the editor and opinion pieces tied to specific initiatives in your local area that are impacted by questions of social justice. Does your community have a living wage campaign? Consider joining with an organization in your area that engages in justice-oriented activities in order to amplify your efforts and build community.

Consider starting an economic accountability prayer group. There are a number of these small groups in the United States and beyond who come together around the "Household Sabbath Economics Covenant."[16] They inventory their own household economies, learn about more just ways of structuring their economics, and help support one another as they implement changes or face setbacks.

Go back once again and review the actions of the early church that are reported above. Virtually every congregation in the United States is near or in a community that has economic needs. A great deal of work is yet to be done before "justice rolls down like the waters," which means the opportunities are myriad. We have given only a couple examples of ways to get more actively involved with issues of economic justice. There are more in the appendix. Pick out one that holds personal interest and start there.

DAY 7 — Group Meeting and Reflection

1. How does lack of access to adequate food, clean water, housing, health care, and other basic necessities of life contribute to conflict and violence? How might this be corrected?

2. What Bible passages do you remember about God's concern for those on the margins of our society? What do you think God's expectations for us are with regard to these concerns (both at the personal and public levels)? What steps would you suggest to begin to live into those expectations?

3. What do you think Jesus had in mind when he commented that we will always have the poor with us? Put the claim in its broader biblical context. (Deuteronomy 15, for example, observes that there should be "no poor among you.")

4. What are some popular caricatures of people who live in poverty—from politicians and in the culture? If you had a chance to speak to political leaders or the producers of TV shows, movies, or music that portrays poor people, what would you say to them?

5. *God's Politics* critiques a common perception of capitalism, as in the quote by former Treasury Secretary O'Neill, regarding the risk/consequence nature of the economic system (page 259). Discuss the critique; and if you find it correct, discuss ways to hold monied interests more accountable.

6. *God's Politics* notes that CEOs have an obligation "to the common good, not just to the bottom line" (page 264). From a Christian perspective, how might we define "common good"? On what, as Christians, would we base such a definition?

7. Assume you were going to make a presentation to a group of wealthy business-people on the notion of economic justice. What are the four or five primary points that you would make?

8. Review the Millennium Development Goals. What has your church done to elevate awareness of these goals? What could be done to increase Christian awareness and response to the Millennium Development Goals?

9. Where does your church invest its money? Does it invest in socially screened funds and community development banking institutions that serve the poor?[17]

10. Discuss the "Top Ten Facts" on international trade (*God's Politics*, page 279). How do trade agreements impact you? As people of faith, do we identify ourselves first with others of our faith across the world, or do we identify ourselves first as Americans? How might this impact how we view trade policies?

11. *God's Politics* says, "For the first time in history we have the information, knowledge, technology, and resources to bring the worst of global poverty to an end. What we don't have is the moral and political will to do so" (page 270). Do you agree? If so, what might we do to help create the moral and political will?

Poverty

IN THE PREVIOUS CHAPTER, we covered economic justice, a broader topic than our current theme—poverty. The relationship between the two is obvious: when economic systems are not just, poverty is one of the most insidious results. Please be sure to review chapters 13 through 15 of *God's Politics* as you work through this material. The following paragraphs provide brief summaries of each chapter.

Chapter 13: Thousands of Bible verses affirm our obligation to care for the poor. Despite this clear and abundant teaching, some people try to argue that when Jesus said, "The poor you will have always with you" (Matthew 26:11), it somehow provided justification for doing little or nothing about poverty—as if Jesus had said there would always be poor people among us, so why do anything about it? However, this misreads both the immediate and the broader contexts of his words. First, this verse comes after Jesus's anointing by the woman at Bethany, prior to his death on the cross—Jesus will not be among the disciples for much longer: "You will not always have me." Second, Jesus is making a judgment about the social location of his followers—that to follow Jesus means we will always have the opportunity, and the gift, of working on behalf of those he called "the least of these."

Chapter 14: The sheer frequency of such verses makes it clear that poverty is a central moral concern for Christians. Thirty-seven million Americans live beneath the official poverty line, and even families that earn just above that level of income have trouble affording life's essentials. Neither of the two major political parties prioritizes the needs of the poor—indeed, the poor often seem little more than pawns in the partisan political debate. Given God's concern for those on the margins of society, we as Christians must ally ourselves with the voiceless millions.

Chapter 15: Jesus once commented that where our treasures are, there our hearts will be also. Similarly, the manner in which a family, church, city, or nation budgets its resources reveals its true priorities—what it loves and what sorts of things it values. When money goes for warfare or tax cuts at the expense of those on the margins, it reveals that our vision of the common good excludes others. The budgets we make and support have consequences—either by making the economic playing field more level and just or by making it less so. We cannot avoid the conclusion that budgets are moral documents and should be assessed by Christians on the basis of how they protect the interests of those most at risk.

DAY 1 — Introducing the Topic

We are all familiar with the term "poverty," but how many of us have reflected on what the term really means—and, more important, on what living in poverty is like? Poverty means not having access to the basic essentials of life, including (among others) food, shelter, clothing, and health care.

Think about what this means. If you are living at or below the poverty level—where you do not have access to the bare essentials of life—you will not be making trade-offs between, say, eating at a fast-food place or a sit-down restaurant for dinner. Nor will you be deciding between that three-bedroom brick house with two and a half baths and an entertainment room or a four-bedroom house with a detached garage and three baths. No, the trade-offs you will be facing will be more like putting a roof over your family's head versus having health care. Or maybe you will be fortunate and have both today, but your spouse will have to quit taking medications for a few days. In other words, the trade-offs are about which life essentials you will give up. And if you happen to have a child with a chronic health problem, any chance of getting ahead is traded for the hope of just getting by.

A popular stereotype of the person living in poverty is someone who just doesn't want to work or who can't hold down a job. But such stereotypes miss the fact that children are among those most exposed to poverty. The stereotype is mistaken in another way, as it increasingly is the case that many of those who live below the poverty line are also employed.

It's difficult to find work that pays reasonably well and is also within walking distance of affordable housing. Thus in order to work, a person needs transportation. Of course, folks with few financial resources can rarely afford to own reliable transportation. Unless you live in an area with a good mass-transit system, you will have to come up with the money to buy a vehicle. Don't forget that you will also need to pay vehicle taxes and registration fees, maintain a fund for repairs, and acquire enough money for at least liability insurance—as well as gas. Mass transit, if available and close by, may be less expensive, but you will need to adjust your schedule to fit the transit schedule. And if you have children, to be able to hold a job you will need to make enough money—beyond food, shelter, and clothing—to cover child care.

It's common for single parents to leave home before sunrise and travel for more than an hour to a job where the level of pay provides little or no genuine opportunity to get ahead, or even to catch up. Repeating the long travel in the evening, those parents may face the dark before they return home. In the meantime, children have been left either on their own or with grandparents (if they are close by), or have been taken to child care. Many Christians have expressed concern about the breakdown of the family. Yet many of us remain too quiet when it comes to establishing social policies and public institutions to address poverty and to support the kinds of efforts that truly help families be strong.

The moral of the story is this: work is not working for many. It is not generating enough income for poor families to escape the circumstances that poverty creates and reinforces. To see why that might be the case, consider that the current poverty level for a family of four in the United States is $19,350. Any family with an income level below that amount is living in poverty. If one of the adults is working full-time at a minimum-wage job, and that person is the only wage earner, the family income will be $10,712, or just over 50 percent of the poverty level. If both parents work at that type job, the total income will be $21,424. However, given that both parents will be out of the house, some of that money—often a sizable chunk—will go toward child care. After these expenses, what will be the effective pay rate for the second working parent? Half of minimum wage?

The causes of poverty are much debated, and as *God's Politics* observes, sometimes the debate *about* poverty consumes so much energy that there seems to be little actual progress in alleviating it. Perhaps the two most debated questions are: (1) What are the causes of poverty? and (2) What course of action has the best chance of alleviating it? While it is relatively easy to identify correlations between poverty and particular public policies, establishing a causal link is more difficult. This leaves the poor suffering the agony of the trade-offs noted above, while the policymakers continue the debate. No doubt there is genuine concern on both sides of the political aisle, but it is time to move beyond debate to solutions. People are more important than theories. Rather than engaging the same old debates—such as whether poverty is related mainly to lifestyle or to lack of real economic opportunity and good domestic policies—we need to experiment with creative solutions. For example, we might consider solutions that put the poor and the wealthy in closer proximity, creating more mixed economic neighborhoods and business zones. We primarily need solutions that see the status quo as unacceptable.

We have the ability to end extreme poverty on a global level. The question is whether we have the will. The old "trickle-down" theories have been shown to be bankrupt when it comes to, well, "trickling down." What is most heartbreaking, from a Christian perspective, is how little the church has taken the lead on this issue—the most frequently addressed social issue in the Bible—although thankfully, that is changing.

Extreme poverty is far too common in the majority of the world. More than 1 billion people live on less than $1 per day. Droughts, partially resulting from climate changes brought on by pollution and nonsustainable agricultural practices, have destroyed crops and food supplies in many of the poorest countries. Farm subsidies have contributed to making agriculture unprofitable for poor farmers. International trade is governed by institutions that tilt the playing field in favor of the wealthiest countries. Trade negotiations are driven by those wealthy countries, which use their existing economic and military might to force unfavorable conditions on poorer countries. One cannot help but think of Isaiah 10:1–4, which castigates the lawmakers who prevent the poor and needy from gaining justice.[1] When we enjoy the low prices created by farm subsidies or the exploitation of foreign markets, to what extent do we participate in the poverty to which these policies contribute?

DAY 2   Considering the Evidence

Before we turn our attention to current facts and statistics on poverty, let's look at the history of the last 100 years in the United States to see how the issue of poverty has changed. The pre–Civil War economy was based on the most dire system of oppression possible, of course: actual slavery. The late 1800s and early 1900s saw a laissez-faire American economic system: there was little government regulation, and there were virtually no trade unions. Business owners were allowed to do what they deemed appropriate in order to maximize profits. Abuse and exploitation of workers were common. The old Tennessee Ernie Ford song "Sixteen Tons" captured some of that reality:

> Sixteen tons, and what do you get?
> Another day older and deeper in debt
> St. Peter don't you call me, 'cause I can't go
> I owe my soul to the company store.

Company stores were able to price products so that miners never could quite get ahead. The basic essentials cost too much to purchase with their wages, so they borrowed from the store to survive. Unsafe working conditions, child labor, long work days and work weeks, and no time off were part and parcel of the working conditions of many.

This fostered a "trickle-up" economics that allowed ever-increasing accumulations of wealth for a few at the top. The gap that opened between the poorest Americans and the richest Americans, along with the economic instability these conditions invited, created a big problem. As we know, the bottom fell out of the U.S. economy in the late 1920s, and the country found itself in the midst of the Great Depression. It is estimated that the mid-1930s saw a poverty rate of nearly 50 percent in the United States: half of all Americans could not obtain the basic essentials of life. By 1940, an estimated one-third of Americans were in poverty.

With the election of Franklin Delano Roosevelt in 1932 and the institution of the New Deal, a serious attempt was made to use national and state institutions to solve the problem of poverty. At the time, one of the highest poverty rates was among the elderly. The introduction of Social Security began to reduce significantly the number of elderly living in poverty. Through the 1940s and 1950s, the poverty rate steadily declined, until by 1965 it was just over 15 percent. During this period, the gap between the poorest and the wealthiest grew very little, and the growing prosperity of the middle class became the country's economic driving force.

In 1965, Lyndon Johnson launched the "war on poverty," and the poverty rate continued to decline until it reached a low in 1973 of just over 11 percent. Since then the level of poverty assistance (adjusted for inflation) has declined, and the poverty rate has fluctuated; in late 2005 the rate was just under 13 percent. The lesson: poverty rates are impacted positively by public-sector intervention. And they are impacted negatively when the public sector fails to take appropriate steps to reduce wealth inequality and to protect those on the margins.

The United States' current poverty rate of 12.7 percent equals about 37 million Americans living below the poverty line. Thirteen million of those in poverty are children—in fact, 17.8 percent of all children live below the poverty line.[2] Children have always constituted a disproportionate share of those in poverty.

Access to health care is among the essentials most quickly lost by those living in poverty. Estimates indicate that 45 million Americans are without health insurance. Recently, Congress cut Medicaid and similar programs in order to fund tax cuts for the wealthiest and the war in Iraq, making it even more difficult for poor people to access adequate health care.

It is generally estimated that, in most areas of the country, an amount double the poverty rate is actually needed to live. Consider the following hypothetical budget for a family of four living at the poverty rate of $19,350:

Housing	$8,100/year ($675/month)
Utilities	$1,200/year ($100/month)
Food	$8,760/year ($2 per person per meal)
Transportation	$2,860/year ($55/week, public transit or low-cost car and insurance)
Clothing	$1,600/year ($400 per person per year, secondhand)
Social Security taxes	$ 1,480
Total expenses	$24,000

We are already more than $4,000 over budget! What are we going to cut to get to $19,350? You could avoid most transportation costs if you walked to work, except you would still need to get groceries and other items home. Besides, what are the chances of finding work close to home? The closer to town, the higher the rent. You could cut the whole $4,000 excess if you figured out how to cut the average meal to $1 per meal per person per day. If you rented housing on or near a farm, you might be able to raise some vegetables or fruits. For most people, however, the prospects aren't good. Ron Sider invites us to reflect on what is not included in this budget:

> No household appliances, no vacations, no toiletries, no birthday or Christmas gifts, no recreation, no visits to the dentist, no private health insurance, no donations for church, no child care, no movies, no travel outside the city, no private music lessons, no sports equipment for the children. Poor people, of course, do have some of these things. However unthinkable from a middle-class perspective, somehow they manage to spend less on some of the other items or receive help from family, friends, or church.[3]

Take a look at your own budget, compare the two, and then ask what you would have to give up to live at the poverty level.

Consider the following statistics[4] regarding the assets of the wealthiest Americans and ask yourself, "As a Christian, can I continue to support public policies that result in such inequality?" If your answer is no, how might those policies be corrected?

Distribution of Wealth Ownership, 2001

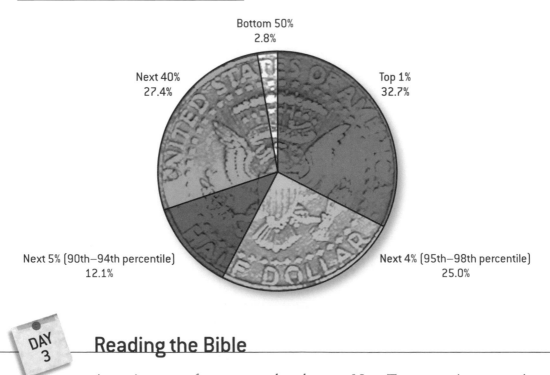

Bottom 50%
2.8%

Next 40%
27.4%

Top 1%
32.7%

Next 5% (90th–94th percentile)
12.1%

Next 4% (95th–98th percentile)
25.0%

DAY 3 — Reading the Bible

A seminary professor started a class on New Testament interpretation with the question, "What is the most disbelieved verse in the Bible?" Fearing a setup, students were slow to respond. The professor continued, "The passage in Mark 10, where Jesus says it is impossible for a rich man to enter the kingdom of heaven." Most of the students were taken by surprise, but the professor went on to explain: "Because we are so wealthy, we Americans have only two choices. We could give up our wealth for the poor. Or we could interpret this passage in a way that holds it at arm's length, making it about motivations or attitudes. It can be about anything except what we are obliged to do with our wealth."

God expresses genuine and consistent concern for the poorest in society—and that concern begins long before the teaching and preaching of Jesus. In *God's Politics,* we read that there are more than 2,000 verses in the Bible that deal with the poor and with God's commands regarding them.

For example, we find the following in Exodus: "If you lend money to my people, to the poor among you, you shall not deal with them as a creditor; you shall not exact interest from them" (22:25). God's concern for the precarious existence of the poor leads God to expect different treatment for the poor than for the non-poor. In the next few verses in Exodus, God makes it clear that we are not intended to act dishonestly to protect the poor, but we should make the protection of the poor an integral part of establishing just social institutions.

Of course, God fully realizes we have a tendency to be self-centered. This is explicit in the following earlier-quoted passage: "Since there will never cease to be some in need on the earth, I therefore command you, 'Open your hand to the poor and needy neighbor in your land'" (Deuteronomy 15:11).

Many suggest that we cannot do anything about the condition of the poor. In the above passage, however, God commands us to keep our hands open to provide for the poor. Deuteronomy 15 also includes the command to observe years of debt release every seven years, when all debts are to be forgiven.

These commands are not to be taken merely as guidelines for individuals, to be voluntarily obeyed by one person or another, but corporate commands. Consider, for example, that God frequently includes the warning of punishment for failure to obey:

> May the Lord defend the cause of the poor of the people, give deliverance to the needy, and crush the oppressor. (Psalm 72:4)

> Hear this, you that trample on the needy, and bring to ruin the poor of the land, saying, "When will the new moon be over so that we may sell grain; and the sabbath, so that we may offer wheat for sale? We will make the ephah small and the shekel great, and practice deceit with false balances, buying the poor for silver and the needy for a pair of sandals, and selling the sweepings of the wheat."

> The Lord has sworn by the pride of Jacob: Surely I will never forget any of their deeds. Shall not the land tremble on this account, and everyone mourn who lives in it. (Amos 8:4–8)

> Ah, you who make iniquitous decrees, who write oppressive statutes, to turn aside the needy from justice and to rob the poor of my people of their right, that widows may be your spoil, and that you may make the orphans your prey! What will you do on the day of punishment, in the calamity that will come from far away? To whom will you flee for help, and where will you leave your wealth . . . ? (Isaiah 10:1–3)

It is clear God is concerned about the exploitation of the poor. Virtually everyone would agree with this. But millions of people remain in poverty, and the poor continue to be exploited. Why?

Most of us likely do not see the effects our choices have on poor individuals or families or communities. We think that because we do not hold slaves or force workers to take low-wage jobs, we are not part of the problem. But is it so simple? If we buy products from companies known to run sweatshops, aren't we complicit with the executives that run them? Aren't we supporting and affirming their policies? When we support legislation, do we encourage our elected representatives to support poverty relief? Do we support living wage movements? Few of us openly exploit the poor. However, we must also consider the consequences of our choices—particularly their impact on the marginalized.

Just as the Bible warns us about exploiting and abusing the poor, so it encourages us to engage in actions that benefit the poor: "Those who despise their neighbors are sinners, but happy are those who are kind to the poor" (Proverbs 14:21). "Those who oppress the poor insult their Maker, but those who are kind to the needy honor God" (Proverbs 14:31). "Whoever is kind to the poor lends to the Lord, and will be repaid in full" (Proverbs 19:17). "Those who are generous are blessed, for they share their bread with the poor" (Proverbs 22:9). "If you wish to be perfect, go, sell your possessions, and give the money to the poor, and you will have treasure in heaven; then come, follow me" (Matthew 19:21). And from Isaiah:

> Is not this the fast that I choose: to loose the bonds of injustice, to undo the thongs of the yoke, to let the oppressed go free, and to break every yoke? Is it not to share your bread with the hungry, and bring the homeless poor into your house; when you see the naked, to cover them, and not to hide yourself from your own kin? (58:6–7)

In all these passages we see the extent to which God offers blessing to those who take up the cause of the poor. Why? Because being mindful of those in need is an expression of God's own nature.

In short, God intends that there be no poor, while God realizes that our self-centeredness will make it such that we will always have the poor among us. To be imitators of God, however, we must join God in coming to the defense of the poor. This must be true both in our personal acts of mercy and in our support of public institutions and policies that incorporate protections for the poor. The biblical call to live modestly and to understand our wealth as a gift from God (not a right or a prize for our righteous or smart actions) means that all must take seriously care for the poor.

A foundational biblical principle is that every single human life has a fundamental dignity, because we are all created in the image of God. This is largely connected to our human purpose of being made for relationships with God and with each other. Few things rob humans of their dignity more than poverty. We must engage with each other in ways that defend human dignity, an obligation that includes addressing the root causes and consequences of poverty.

We close with an admonition from Corinthians:

> I do not mean that there should be relief for others and pressure on you, but it is a question of a fair balance between your present abundance and their need, so that their abundance may be for your need, in order that there may be a fair balance. As it is written, "The one who had much did not have too much, and the one who had little did not have too little." (2 Corinthians 8:13–15)

DAY 4 — The Christian Tradition

It's not surprising that poverty is closely connected to issues relating to a just economy. It is most often injustices within economies that contribute to a breakdown in community, which results in some people being unable to obtain the bare essentials. In other words, if we take seriously the words of the previous biblical verses, we would restructure our economy to be more just for "the least of these." Of course, restructuring threatens to restrict the ability of those in power to accumulate without limit, so there would be resistance. Let's look at some teachings from the early church that relate to our concern for those in poverty.

Consider these words from a second-century Christian writing called the Didache:

> Do not be one who holds his hand out to take, but shuts it when it comes to giving. If your labor has brought you earnings, pay a ransom for your sins. Do not hesitate to give and do not give with a bad grace, for you will discover who [God] is that pays you back a reward with a good grace. Do not turn your back on the needy, but share everything with your brother [and sister] and call nothing your own. For if you have what is eternal in common, how much more should you have what is transient![5]

Notice again the connection between helping the needy and seeing them as part of your family. All are now united under God, and our obligations to the poor are analogous to family obligations.

Basil the Great, a theologian who lived and worked during the fourth century, was concerned for the poor and recognized the obligations the rich have toward them:

> "Whom do I injure," [the rich person] says, "when I retain and conserve my own?" ... Such are the rich. Because they were first to occupy common goods, they take these goods as their own. If each one would take that which is sufficient for one's needs, leaving what is in excess to those in distress, no one would be rich, no one poor.... Is God unjust to distribute the necessaries of life to us unequally? Why are you rich, why is that one poor? Is it not that you may receive the reward of beneficence and faithful distribution ...?[6]

In a classic sermon to the rich, St. Basil explained that when some have more than others, it is their obligation to use their wealth to help others:

> That bread which you keep, belongs to the hungry; that coat which you preserve in your wardrobe, to the naked; those shoes which are rotting in your possession, to the shoeless; that gold which you have hidden in the ground, to the needy. Wherefore, as often as you were able to help others, and refused, so often did you do them wrong.[7]

Could there be a clearer statement than this—that what we have in excess of our basic needs belongs to the poor and hungry? St. Basil doesn't even grant that the giving of excess is worthy of praise; if it is excess, *it already belongs to the poor.*

Finally, consider a piece from St. John Chrysostom. In it, he speculates on what could be done if we lived as we're called to in Acts 2:

> Let us imagine things as happening in this way: All give all that they have into a common fund. No one would have to concern himself about it, neither the rich nor the poor. How much money do you think would be collected? I infer—for it cannot be said with certainty—that if every individual contributed all his money, his lands, his estates, his houses ... then a million pounds of gold would be obtained, and most likely two or three times that amount.... And how many of the poor do we have? I doubt that there are more than 50,000. How much would be required to feed them daily? If they all ate at a common table, the cost could not be very great. What could we not undertake with our huge treasure! Do you believe it could ever be exhausted?
>
> And will not the blessing of God pour down on us a thousand-fold richer? Will we not make a heaven on earth? Would not the grace of God be indeed richly poured out?[8]

Here John not only depends on the beneficence of Constantinople's wealthy, but also suggests that God would richly bless those living out God's intentions.

As we can see, these early Christians did not defend the right of the rich to have all they could get. They were more interested in reminding the wealthy of the serious obligations their wealth carries.

DAY 5 ## Living Examples in the Contemporary Church

Christian churches could make an immediate and drastic impact on resolving domestic and global poverty if they committed themselves to that task. Public and private sectors have a role to play in poverty relief, and it is good to see churches becoming increasingly active in charity (through soup kitchens and food pantries) and justice (in their attempts to influence public policy). In the following vignette, we see how the *personal* nature of faith finds *outward* expression in Chicago's New Community Covenant Church.

FAITH: NOT A PRIVATE PRACTICE

Pastor Peter Hong asserts that Chicago's New Community Covenant Church "exists to provide an alternative to those tired of religion." But the four-year-old, ethnically diverse congregation certainly embraces its identity as both spiritual and religious. "So much of what has gone wrong in the evangelical community is this notion that the Christian faith is a private faith," says Hong. "It may begin as a personal faith, but it was never meant to be a private faith."

This distinction describes well a church equally invested in the spiritual lives of individuals and in its religious role as a corporate and communal body. Community is an underlying value of all the congregation's ministries, from service- and fellowship-oriented small groups to lay-led prayer before Sunday worship. Hong notes the closeness of the words "community" and "communion," a theological connection echoed by fellowship team leader Olivia Littles: "We talk about how Christ's death and resurrection reconciled us not only to Christ but also to the world."

New Community does more than talk about such doctrines. It strives to respond to Christ's apostolic call to geographically concentric circles of ministry, from local to global, because, as Hong explains, "we believe that this is where the heart of God is." The congregation is involved in international missions; it also runs a warming center a few blocks from the church office. The latter began three winters ago as an outgrowth of ad hoc ministry to neighborhood homeless people. A homeless acquaintance asked church staff member Katie Sandford where the nearest warming center was; Sandford and other staff responded by creating one. The largely volunteer-run facility now serves more than thirty people daily, providing daytime access to material supplies, communications, and social services referrals. "Most important," says Sandford, "people are treated with dignity and respect."

These same values motivated the multiethnic and justice-seeking team of women and men that founded New Community. The church has since outgrown multiple worship spaces and added a second service, bearing witness to its identity as an alternative not to religion itself so much as to irrelevant or inadequate expressions of religion. Hong sees New Community as part of a broader trend toward a faith both personal and communal, of a "transition from the old paradigm to a new one."

STEVE THORNGATE*

There are other churches where sermons and Sunday school classes focus on ways to become directly involved in outreach to those on the margins. Some churches, for example, have a class that alternates Sundays between in-church Bible study and community-based relief efforts: one week they have a traditional Sunday school class focused thematically or on a specific book of the Bible; the next they travel to local community outreach centers, help organize food pantries, or participate in an inner-city church service. Participants have found that the practice of ministerial outreach complements and deepens the study experiences on alternate weekends. Virtually any church could imitate this model.

DAY 6 — Putting Faith into Action

No area in the United States is beyond the reach of poverty. Hungry children are almost certainly within a short drive of your home. This means that opportunities to make a difference in the fight against poverty are also nearby. There are a variety of ways to engage peace and justice struggles—particularly those related to poverty—and many involve concrete opportunities for "hands-on" work.

Many churches and parachurch organizations maintain a variety of ministries for those who need help making ends meet. In addition, there are secular soup kitchens, food and clothing banks, and shelters that take in the homeless and provide meals and a place to sleep for the night. These facilities are constantly in need of help—from food servers and dishwashers to facility organizers and good repair people. You can also donate food, extra clothing, or cash. For Christians it is necessary to build relationships of love, care, and support with those who are struggling, not just give money from arm's length. You might also consider working with your church to develop its own outreach ministry for those in need in your community.

Many of the opportunities identified in the appendix are also applicable here. Few people realize the depths of poverty, either in the United States or internation-

---

* *Steve Thorngate is an editorial assistant at* Sojourners. *From* Sojourners, *December 2005, vol. 34, no. 11, p. 15.*

ally. Consequently, it is critical to develop and use good educational resources. For example, you might put together a series on "the face of poverty" and "the face of wealth." You could present key statistics on poverty and wealth so that members of your congregation might begin to see the demographics of economic disparity. In the course of any educational program, it will be important to show the biblical and theological connections. Conduct a "live in poverty" exercise where the group develops a budget based on what a family could afford to buy on a poverty-level budget. It would be worth discussing what is and is not included in the budget. What has been left out to make ends meet? Perhaps your group could agree to live by that budget for a week or a month. With an exercise like this, it is important to debrief afterward. Discuss what insights you have gained. Another exercise is inviting participants to write a "money journal" that details the messages they were given around money as a child and how that background impacts their view of money today.

There are many excellent conferences and events around the country that deal with different aspects of poverty and wealth. Consider attending one by yourself or with others from your church or community.

DAY 7 — Group Meeting and Reflection

1. What role might government play in securing justice for the poor? What role might the church play?

2. Develop a plan for improving the statistics shown on page 223 in *God's Politics* over the next five years.

3. Identify five facts related to poverty that you think most reflect the severity of the problem. Identify five facts related to wealth that you think most reflect the severity of the problem.

4. What are some of the underlying causes of extreme poverty and excessive wealth? How would you set about tackling some of those causes?

5. Does the biblical notion of "aliens" (Leviticus 19:33–34) and the commands God gave regarding them guide us in developing a Christian immigration policy? If so, what would that policy look like?

6. Discuss what *God's Politics* means in its claim that budgets are moral documents. How would you try to make this point to your friends?

7. Go to www.whitehouse.gov/omb/budget/fy2007/ and review the U.S. budget. Imagine you are asked to testify before Congress on the moral implications of the existing budget, but you have only ten minutes to make your presentation. What points would you try to make?

8. Do you agree with *God's Politics'* assessment that the biblical prophets would be very critical of the Bush administration's budget priorities? Why or why not?

9. Why has the repeal of the federal estate tax become such a hot-ticket item for many conservatives? Consider the intent behind the years of jubilee and years of debt release in Leviticus 25 and Deuteronomy 15. Comment on how these passages speak to a possible repeal of the estate tax.

10. Assess the validity of *Washington Post* columnist E. J. Dionne's concern (addressed in *God's Politics*, pages 251–252) about the Bush administration's faith-based initiatives.

11. What should twenty-first-century Christians do about the biblical notion of economic "leveling" that *God's Politics* talks about? What are ways the jubilee message could be brought into the twenty-first century?

A Consistent Ethic of Life

I**N WEEK 5,** we turn our attention to discussing a consistently pro-life position. The term "pro-life" has been largely equated with the opposition to abortion. But *God's Politics* argues in chapter 18 that a consistent ethic in support of life cannot be focused on a single issue. Familiarize yourself with chapter 18, and read below the brief summary of the chapter's definition and defense of a consistent ethic of life.

Chapter 18: Catholic Cardinal Joseph Bernardin of Chicago coined the phrase "a seamless garment of life," linking a number of issues related to the defense of life—abortion, euthanasia, capital punishment, nuclear weapons, poverty, and racism.[1] A consistently pro-life position must bring each of these components into a holistic ethic of life. Too often, promoting a culture of life has focused only on banning abortion. On this issue, the Left tends to exclude those who are opposed to abortion, while the Right tends to narrow the pro-life discussion so that it includes almost nothing besides abortion.

DAY 1   Introducing the Topic

"Pro-life." "Pro-choice." These are two labels with which Americans are well acquainted. Unfortunately, both tend to be used more for their bumper-sticker value than to promote substantive dialogue or to convey a consistent and sophisticated position. We need to move beyond the false dichotomy set up by these two phrases and embrace instead a position more holistically grounded in unapologetic and unconditional support for human life and well-being.

Those on the political Right are correct in insisting that abortion is a moral issue and should not be considered just another form of birth control. At the same time, those on the Left are correct in defending the dignity of women and in saying that simply criminalizing abortion will not create a culture of life. Some have argued that abortion should be "safe, legal, and rare," but often little is done to realize the third leg of this proposed triangle. So where does this leave us? As people of God, what can we learn from our tradition as we embrace the goal of valuing each and every life?

When Cardinal Bernardin used the phrase "seamless garment of life," he intended an unconditional embrace of life across a whole range of issues, as noted above, including abortion, euthanasia, capital punishment, war, nuclear weapons, poverty, and racism. By this standard, to be pro-life only in the sense of being opposed to abortion is to be *conditionally* pro-life: if the life in question is that of an unborn child, then one is for defending that life. Bernardin suggests that we must not allow our defense of life to be so narrowly focused. Let's consider briefly some of the issues listed above.

For example, how do we understand capital punishment in terms of a consistent ethic of life? The number of executions in the United States has decreased in recent years, according to the Death Penalty Information Center, as has citizen support for capital punishment. One of the major reasons is the increasing concern that innocent people may be sentenced to death. Since 1973, 119 people in 25 states have been exonerated and released from death row because of evidence of their innocence. As these cases have received national exposure, more Americans have come to question the institution of capital punishment.[2]

"Honorable people have disagreed about the justice of executing the guilty," writes Catholic sister Helen Prejean in her book *The Death of Innocents: An Eyewitness Account of Wrongful Executions,* "but can anyone argue about the justice of executing the innocent?"

Of particular interest to Christians is Prejean's account of recent developments in the Catholic tradition's position on capital punishment. In his 1995 encyclical *Evangelium Vitae* (Gospel of Life), Pope John Paul II stated that even murderers possess human dignity and the practice of the death penalty should therefore be "rare, if not nonexistent" in modern societies. While some theologians argue that capital punishment is permitted in rare cases in defense of society against an imminent threat to citizens' lives, the Catholic Church now stands in principled opposition to the death penalty. "The entire argument for self-defense changes ... when violent offenders are incarcerated and thereby rendered defenseless," writes Prejean. "Where, then, is the threat of an immediate violent assault on citizens?"

Prejean also articulates the principled theological argument against the death penalty when she shows how Christian misunderstandings of atonement lead some to an inappropriate support of capital punishment. She believes that the traditional satisfaction theory of atonement contributes to Christians' support of the death penalty, and she calls this theology into question: "Is God vengeful, demanding a death for a death? Or is God compassionate, luring souls into love so great that no one can be considered 'enemy'?"

Ultimately, for Christians who believe that Jesus preached a way of nonviolence, the teachings of Karl Barth and John Howard Yoder are critical. Both argue that since Jesus was the victim of a state-sponsored execution, no Christian can support this mechanism as a just means of preserving social order for either the innocent or the guilty.

We have already discussed Christian responses to war and peace in Week 2. A consistently pro-life position would take a strong stance against war and work in whatever means possible to support nonviolent ways to resolve injustice and conflict internationally and within countries as well.

We must also consider the continuing destruction of our environment as part of a "life stance." There is widespread agreement that global warming is endangering our quality of life on the earth, that the rainforest is declining at an alarming rate, and that our dependence on fossil fuels is becoming an insupportable strain on the environment. A consistent and wide-ranging ethic of life must make care for the environment a central concern.

Poverty and racism are also concerns that fit into a consistent ethic of life. These are addressed in detail in Weeks 4 and 6. A consistently pro-life position must also include the goal of affordable health care for all people. Every day, individuals are forced to make trade-offs between food and life-saving medicines, between needed health procedures and housing. More than 45 million Americans have no health insurance, and a disproportionate number of these are children. Concern for these issues is essential to a broader pro-life position.

Additionally, a pro-life stance must examine nuclear weapons. The United States is the only country to have used nuclear weapons against a civilian population. When the U.S. dropped nuclear weapons on Japan in World War II, more than 300,000 Japanese died, and 95 percent of them were civilians. Nuclear weapons cause indiscriminate mass annihilation. They are tools of terror. By their very nature they violate the moral principles of justice, discrimination, and proportionality that are laid out in the just war principles we examined earlier. Nearly all major Christian churches, and many Jewish and Muslim bodies, have spoken out against nuclear weapons—encouraging support to freeze, lockdown, and eliminate nuclear weapons.

"So-called realists," writes David Cortright of the Fourth Freedom Forum, "claim that the advocates of nuclear abolition are utopians. On the contrary, the naive utopians are those who believe that governments can maintain nuclear weapons in perpetuity without their actual use, either by accident or design. As former Defense Secretary Robert McNamara has said, the indefinite combination of human fallibility and continued reliance on nuclear weapons will lead to catastrophe and the destruction of cities."[3]

Nuclear abolition is realistic. Treaties against biological and chemical weapons already exist, and it is past time for a similar ban on nuclear weapons. "Only God has the authority to end all life on the planet," writes William Sloane Coffin in opposing nuclear weapons. "All we have is the power." It is time to relinquish that power, to serve rather than usurp God by preserving life.

In the next section, we will take a look at some of the statistics related to these areas, in order to better grasp the serious nature of each. For now let's summarize the positions that might constitute a consistent ethic in support of life.

- Specific plans aimed at genuinely and significantly reducing the number of abortions should be put into place. These must include steps to promote availability of health care and nutrition for mothers and children, improve and streamline adoption processes, and reduce child poverty.
- A platform of restorative justice for those convicted of committing crimes should be developed. Such a platform must hold offenders accountable and demand reparation for victims while also seeking reconciliation with victims and the restoration of human dignity to everyone involved. The public must be educated on the ineffectiveness of capital punishment. It does not serve as a deterrent to capital crimes (even the U.S. Justice Department shows no correlation between executions and a reduction in violent offenses); it is more expensive than life in prison; and it is irreversible. This last point is especially important when we factor in the fallibility of the criminal justice system, the inherent racism in that system, and the unequal access to a credible defense because of income.
- The use of nuclear weapons—in any circumstance—must be taken off the table. The international community must conduct multilateral negotiations to reduce the number of nuclear devices in military stockpiles and develop a reliable means of policing. The United States will have to lead and be willing to expose itself to the same tests expected of other countries.
- We must aggressively pursue protection of the earth's resources and the care and well-being of humans as part of biosystems. We must consider the long-term effects of our energy choices, manufacturing policies, wasteful lifestyles, etc. It makes little sense to defend the unborn unless we also take care to ensure that they will have a healthy environment in which to flourish.
- Poverty and racism must be eliminated. Both exclude people from resources—social, psychological, and material—and a consistent ethic of life does not allow for such exclusion.
- Finally, because it values the sanctity of all lives, a consistently pro-life position works for a reduction in the use of violence to settle international disputes, leading to the abolition of all war, and in the meantime actively pursues the "things that make for peace" (Luke 19:42).

DAY 2 | Considering the Evidence

A consistently pro-life position must fundamentally address the issue most often associated with the term: abortion. Such a position would include steps aimed at reducing the number of pregnancies terminated. According to the Alan Guttmacher Institute (the leading source of abortion statistics), the number of abortions per year in the United States reached a high in 1990 of more than 1.6 million.

The number then declined throughout the 1990s and dropped to just under 1.3 million by 2000. Since then, it has begun to rise slightly. The institute suggests that the biggest contributor to declining abortion rates has been increased education about and availability of contraceptives. Also, since abortion rates have increased significantly among poor women, focused efforts to improve economic conditions among the poor will likely further reduce abortions.

From 1972 to 2004, there were more than 40 million abortions in the United States. In a single year, 1995, there were approximately 26 million legal and 20 million illegal abortions worldwide, resulting in a worldwide abortion rate of 35 per 1,000 women aged 15 to 44. Among the subregions of the world, Eastern Europe had the highest abortion rate (90 per 1,000) and Western Europe the lowest rate (11 per 1,000). Among countries where abortion is legal without restriction, the highest abortion rate, 83 per 1,000, was reported for Vietnam and the lowest, 7 per 1,000, for Belgium and the Netherlands. Abortion rates are no lower overall in areas where abortion is generally restricted by law (and where many abortions are performed under unsafe conditions) than in areas where abortion is legally permitted.[4]

Who has abortions? Statistics show that the profile of a woman in the United States seeking an abortion is young (54 percent under age 24), never married (54 percent), poor or low-income (57 percent under 200 percent of the poverty line), and minority (52 percent African American or Latino).[5] The major reasons given by women seeking abortions are that they cannot afford a child and that they lack health care for themselves and their children. Thus some abortions could be prevented by making health care and other needed support more widely available to mothers and infants. A consistent ethic of life cannot reduce concern for the life of children after they are born.

A group of members of Congress, working with the Democrats for Life organization, are preparing a package of legislative proposals that would actually do something to address the conditions that lead to abortions. The package includes programs that address appropriate sex education for teenagers, pregnancy counseling, protection of women from domestic violence, and adoption reform; *and* increased funding for pre- and postnatal health care, for the Women, Infant, and Children nutrition program, and for other programs that support women and children. Supporters of this legislative package have named it "95-10," because of their goal of reducing the number of abortions by 95 percent in the next ten years. The legislation addresses both the causes of unwanted pregnancies and the need to support infants and their mothers after birth. It's a good example of a common ground initiative that could actually accomplish results rather than further intensifying rhetoric.

Capital punishment is another critical component of a consistently pro-life agenda. What do we need to take into consideration when constructing a consistently pro-life stance with regard to criminal justice? Data from the NAACP Legal Defense Fund's *Death Row USA* for the final quarter of 2005 indicated that the number of people sentenced to death in 2005 was 65 percent fewer than in 1998. The Death Penalty Information Center's analysis of death row population figures from the report showed that 106 people received a death sentence in 2005, down from 125 in 2004 and dramatically lower than the 300 per year recorded in the late 1990s.

Even as the use of the death penalty continued to decline in the United States, the number of murders and the national murder rate dropped in 2004. According to the recently released FBI Uniform Crime Report for 2004, the nation's murder rate fell by 3.3 percent, declining to 5.5 murders per 100,000 people in 2004. In 2004, the number of executions, the number of death sentences, and the size of the death row population all declined compared to 2003.

Additionally, many studies show that lifelong incarceration is less expensive than trying, sentencing, and executing a prisoner. "Every dollar we spend on a capital case is a dollar we can't spend anywhere else.... We have to let the public know what it costs [to pursue a capital case]," said John M. Bailey, Connecticut's chief state's attorney. The death penalty comes at a high price—morally and financially. In Texas, a death penalty case costs taxpayers an average of $2.3 million, about three times the cost of imprisoning someone in a single cell at the highest security level for forty years. In Florida, each execution costs the state $3.2 million. In financially strapped California, one report estimated that the state could save $90 million each year by abolishing capital punishment. The New York Department of Correctional Services estimated that implementing the death penalty would cost the state about $118 million annually.[6]

More important are serious questions about the fair application of the death penalty, as those who are poor and/or minorities are much more likely to be executed than are middle-class whites. According to Amnesty International, even though African Americans and whites are murder victims in nearly equal numbers of crimes in the U.S., 80 percent of people executed since the death penalty was reinstated in the United States have been executed for murders involving white victims. More than 20 percent of black defendants who have been executed were convicted by all-white juries. Biblical evidence leads us away from a "retributive" approach to justice and toward a "restorative" theory of justice. A consistent and unconditional ethic of life must reject capital punishment.

We turn our attention next to the biblical basis for arguing that a consistent ethic of life extends beyond only opposition to abortion to the seamless garment of life of which Cardinal Bernardin spoke.

DAY 3 · Reading the Bible

The Christian tradition affirms that the source of God's creative act is love and overflowing goodness. God creates to bring into existence a world in which

God can share that love with creation. So the creation is filled with living creatures, and it provides an environment for the development of loving relationships among creatures and between God and creatures. A consistent ethic of life is an affirmation of God's intentions for creation and for relationships. In what ways, then, can we affirm that God is "pro-life"?

At every stage of the creation narrative in Genesis, the Bible declares that "God saw it, and it was good." Do we sometimes skip past this too quickly? This simple affirmation is worth some consideration. What is being affirmed, and why is it good? God affirms many things as good: the creation of light, the separation of land from water, the creation of vegetation, the ordering of the world into seasons and into nights and days, the creation of animals—first in the sea, then on land. Finally, God affirms as good the creation of humans as bearers of the image of God. They are good because they conform to the divine intent to build an environment filled with creatures that can love and enjoy their Creator and be loved in return.

There is a special sense of satisfaction expressed on the sixth day. After creating all things, God declares them not just good but "very good." Historically, people have frequently misread passages that warn us not to cling to the world, as if these passages intended us to hate God's creation. A consistent ethic of life must find its starting place in an appropriate appreciation for the created world.

The contemporary "pro-life" movement often uses Deuteronomy 31:19 as its fundamental text: "I set before you today life and death. Choose life." But to use the text simply for that purpose is to miss the richness of what Moses is saying. The book of Deuteronomy is a single presentation of God's instructions, through Moses, to the Israelites. Throughout the Torah (the first five books of the Bible) and especially in Deuteronomy, Moses sets before the people an ethic of life, one characterized by obedience to all instructions given. At the end of the Torah, in the passage in question, Moses readily admits that the people might choose disobedience, which is to "choose death." Moses is pleading with the people, essentially saying, "I have given you God's instructions on how to live. To live in this way is to realize that God's instructions lead to life as God intended. To live contrary to God's intentions is to choose a way that leads to death. I implore you, choose the way of life." It is this "way of life" that undergirds a consistent ethic. Let's look at what the Bible says about some of the specific issues.

There are a number of biblical passages often used in the abortion discussion. "For it was you who formed my inward parts; you knit me together in my mother's womb. I praise you, for I am fearfully and wonderfully made" (Psalm 139:13–14). "Thus says the Lord, your Redeemer, who formed you in the womb: I am the Lord, who made all things" (Isaiah 44:24). And, to the prophet Jeremiah, God says: "Before I formed you in the womb I knew you, and before you were born I consecrated you; I appointed you a prophet to the nations" (Jeremiah 1:5). While these verses do not address abortion, they do articulate a view that life is present before birth.

In Week 2 we took up the question of war: How are we to consider Christian participation in war in light of the Bible's teachings? We cannot affirm war merely on the basis of God's having allowed it in the Old Testament. Instead, we must determine how passages involving God and war are to be read within the overall story of the Bible, with particular attention to the significance of the life and teachings of Jesus.

In Weeks 3 and 4, we examined the issues related to poverty and economic justice. Earlier in Deuteronomy and elsewhere in the Torah, God gives instructions regarding just economies. These include such features as years of release, years of jubilee, gleaning laws, and collateral laws, all aimed to protect the poor and marginalized. There are instructions regarding sanitary habits and crop rotation to protect the earth for future generations. While God affirms a distinction between the chosen people and the rest of the world, the point is the role of the chosen as mediators of God's grace, leaving no room for anything like contemporary racism. All this is included in the "life" that the Israelites must choose.

When it comes to capital punishment, we must consider several factors as we assess the biblical position. Throughout the Bible, God reveals a move away from violent to nonviolent responses to injustice. In some cases, God's seemingly harsh directives exist within an extremely strict honor-code society that used violence to maintain social order. The instruction on proportional punishment—to exact "an eye for an eye" (Exodus 21:24, Leviticus 24:20)—must be situated within the context of the day, which often included the practice of exacting *dis*proportionate revenge against offenders. For example, a group might exact revenge for murder by killing the murderer's entire family. Though "an eye for an eye" sounds to us like an expression of strict judgment, to those to whom it was given "an eye for an eye" was a movement toward reducing and limiting violence.

This movement continues throughout the Bible and reaches its high point in Jesus's teachings and actions. John's gospel (8:3–11) tells the story of a woman caught "in the very act of adultery" (though no mention is made of her equally adulterous partner). She is taken before Jesus by the religious leaders, the keepers of the law of Moses. There is no debate among them about what the law requires. She is to be stoned. Jesus, however, approaches the crisis from another angle. He does not go first to the most obvious and simplistic interpretation of the law of Moses. Instead, he responds in a way that reveals a deeper question about the nature of sin: "He that is without sin among you, let him first cast a stone at her" (John 8:7). Is Jesus setting aside God's clear commands? No. He is simply setting aside proof-texting legalisms and restoring the original heart of mercy to the law. He says in Matthew's gospel: "Think not that I have come to abolish the law, or the prophets: I have come not to abolish, but to fulfill them" (5:17, RSV). Can we see ending capital punishment as, in fact, fulfilling the heart of the biblical law, which is mercy?

We have argued that the progressive revelation of God's expectations is to move us away from seeing violence as a solution to our problems. We also observed that, by instructing people to observe "an eye for an eye," God was moving people in the direction of reducing violence and restoring right relationship. In fact, Jesus deals with the text directly when he says, "You have heard it said, 'An eye for an eye, and a tooth for a tooth': But I say to you, 'That you resist not evil: but whoever smites you on the right cheek, turn to him the other also" (Matthew 5:38–39).

In Romans 12, Paul instructs us to not exact retribution but rather leave this to God: "Beloved, never avenge yourselves, but leave room for the wrath of God; for it is written, 'Vengeance is mine, I will repay, says the Lord.'" A consistent ethic of life, then, cannot include capital punishment based on a retributive theory of justice. Instead, we deal directly with the social and personal crises that violently threaten the community and seek accountability and restoration whenever possible.

DAY 4 — The Christian Tradition

We have used the phrase "consistent ethic of life" to refer to a moral commitment to defend the sanctity of life in a holistic and unconditional fashion. Such a commitment affirms the sanctity of the life of not just the unborn but all people, even our enemies. Consequently, a consistent ethic of life must be concerned about war, poverty, abortion, euthanasia, capital punishment, and racism. Of course, in common usage, a person who claims to be "pro-life" frequently is implying only a position against abortion.

The term "pro-life" was coined in 1973 following the federal Supreme Court decision *Roe vs. Wade,* which overturned all state laws outlawing abortion. Ethics professor David Gushee expresses concern about the term "pro-life," claiming that its evangelical proponents "never have undertaken a full-blown intellectual analysis and exposition, from within our own tradition, of the concept of the sanctity of life."[7] It is toward such "full-blown intellectual analysis" that we point.

The early church took seriously Jesus's injunction to "love our enemies" (Matthew 5:44). Some early church thinkers (Clement of Rome and Justin Martyr, for example) not only opposed Christian participation in war but also denied that a Christian could serve as an executioner. Often they were not so much in debate with the empire about executing criminals as they were working out the implications of the radical change the world had undergone as a result of Jesus's life and teachings. Even if the pagans engaged in execution, those who named Jesus as Lord were not to participate in this practice.

It is clear that the church has had a strong tendency to draw a tight connection between the affirmation that humans are the bearers of God's image and respect for the dignity of life. For example, some expressions of the just war theory are explicit in defending the dignity of the person on the basis of bearing God's image. A detailed examination of the writings of the church would find frequent reference to the theme of honoring the image of God that each of us bears. It is perhaps for this reason that the early church was also opposed to suicide. The surrounding culture seemed to have little problem with suicide—indeed, in some circumstances, suicide was considered an honorable choice. This was not the case within Christianity, however. Oddly, though, there was, within the early church, a notable strand of those who expressed desire for martyrdom. They felt it an honor to suffer for their faith, and death was the ultimate suffering.

By the time we get to the Middle Ages, the church had pretty much universally taken the position that suicide was inconsistent with Christian faith. For example, Thomas Aquinas indicated that suicide was wrong because it violated our innate desire to live, because it harmed others whom we leave behind, and because God, as the giver of life, is the only one who can take life. So, admitting some development over time, it is fair to say that a study of the history of the church indicates that the sanctity of life should lead us to preclude suicide or euthanasia.

In Week 4, we went into some detail about the problem of poverty; in Week 6 we will do the same with racism. Because both of these issues relate to a person's access to life-giving and life-affirming resources, neither can be omitted from a discussion about a consistent ethic of life.

It is clear that the church has tended to draw a tight connection between the affirmation that humans are the bearers of God's image and respect for the dignity of life. For example, some expressions of just war theory explicitly defend the dignity of the individual on the basis of bearing God's image. The writings of the church include many calls to honor the image of God that each of us bears.

There is no doubt that the prevalent view in the history of the church is a condemnation of abortion. The church has tended to err on the side of protecting life and promoting sexual fidelity, rather than come down hard and fast on precisely when personhood begins or the soul enters the flesh. The church's voice has been relatively consistent in its opposition to abortion, although Christian views of how to handle exceptional cases has been a bit more diverse. It is worth noting that before the Enlightenment, the church saw abortion as more a communal sin than an individual one. The termination of a pregnancy signaled a failed marriage or partnership. It signaled that the community was not creating the proper environment where mothers and babies could thrive.

The church has opposed abortion, but it has also been forthright in reminding us of our obligations to the poor and others on the margins. It is hard to say that one has a consistently Christian position on the sanctity of life if one focuses solely on the unborn and leaves the born to fend for themselves. A consistently pro-life position seeks to make abortion rare, defends the human dignity of women, and favors a wide range of services for the care and protection of women, children, and families. A consistently pro-life position does not focus on symptoms without also paying attention to underlying causes. What are the conditions that create hopelessness, which in turn leads some to pursue abortion as a solution to problems? How does lack of adequate health care contribute to a sense of limited choices? How does the ethic of "individualism" lead us to value our own convenience over the life of a child? As we address this range of issues, we move ourselves toward an increasingly consistent ethic of life.

Finally, we should note that people within the church have often spoken of the desensitizing impact a failure to respect life in any of these areas can have on all the others. While some may find capital punishment acceptable because the criminal "deserves" it, state-sanctioned executions contribute to a "culture of death." In *Resident Aliens,* Stanley Hauerwas and Will Willimon ask why we are surprised that the culture that defended its use of atomic weapons against cities in Japan could now come to see abortion as acceptable.[8] War, abortion, capital punishment, poverty, euthanasia, and racism— a position that values the sanctity of human life must address these all.

DAY 5

Living Examples in the Contemporary Church

FINDING ANOTHER WAY:
Abortion Adversaries Seeking Real Solutions

A pro-choice activist describes what it's like when a major pro-life protest occurs in her city: "I'm the one who calls in the army [of volunteer clinic escorts].... It's like a war. I don't like it. I'm tired. I want to see if there's another way to deal with this issue."

So on a brilliant spring day she joined 100 other people in Madison, Wisconsin, in the first national conference of the Common Ground Network for Life and Choice. For four days pro-choice activists, clergy, doctors, and women's clinic directors could be found with pro-life activists, clergy, lawyers, and crisis pregnancy center volunteers in workshops, strategy sessions on teenage pregnancy and adoption, and—perhaps the biggest surprise—friendly conversation.

These people didn't ignore their very real differences on the core issue of abortion, but they also didn't allow those differences to distract them from seeking the "common ground" that exists even among adversaries.

The Common Ground Network came together in 1993 out of dialogue and joint action between pro-choice and pro-life supporters in Buffalo, St. Louis, and elsewhere. The network links such Common Ground groups around the country, providing resources, training, and facilitators.

Activists from both "sides" of the abortion issue sit down together for extended discussion under specified ground rules: respectful speech and behavior; a desire to understand; a pledge to refrain from attempts to convert and convince; and confidentiality.

Discussion moves from issues directly related to abortion (What's the life experience that's led you to the position that you've taken?) to related topics suggested by group members (What are your beliefs about birth control? How do we best teach our children about sexuality?). A goal is to identify areas of agreement and possible cooperative work. Examples have included promoting adoption and developing a mutual "code of conduct" for public hearings concerning abortion.

Participants are not expected to give up their pro-choice or pro-life activism. In between dialogues, they often continue to face each other as adversaries in the media, in city council chambers, or across demonstration lines.

"Common ground" does not mean compromise. While compromise has a rightful place in our society, groups affiliated with the network begin with an understanding that there are core principles on which neither side in the abortion issue conflict can compromise. This doesn't, however, preclude the possibility of civil dialogue and coming together on other principles.

In view of the verbal and physical violence that has characterized the abortion debate in the United States, for adversaries in that debate to meet with listening ears, handshakes, confessions of stereotyping, forgiveness, and statements of basic human respect for one another is not a trivial thing. These groups serve as a needed witness in a country at war with itself on many fronts.

Still, Common Ground groups are not only about people unexpectedly "getting along"—an oddity to be noted and then dismissed. Most participants have a commitment to their communities—a desire that they be safer, more caring places to live, where even sharp disagreements do not bring about violence and torn relationships. They want to see practical changes that increase the resources, justice, equality, *and* choices available to women and families—and many don't see other options.

"I don't think anything else is working, and [Common Ground] is our only chance," said Connie Cook, a pro-choice participant in Common Ground of the Quad Cities (Davenport, Iowa). At the conference one could sense a tangible desire that Common Ground efforts might be like yeast, eventually permeating and changing our country's public discourse on the abortion issue.

Could the Common Ground approach change the way we talk about other issues as well? The Buffalo Coalition for Common Ground has been testing this out, helping to organize, for example, a Common Ground dialogue day for the Presbytery of Western New York on the question of the ordination of gays and lesbians. The coalition is currently planning a day this fall on teen pregnancy, which will bring together people working on the issue, teenagers, and their parents for Common Ground–style conversation.

"This approach requires lots of preliminary work—collecting good data on the topic, making sure you get the right people," says Stan Bratton, one of the founders of the Buffalo Coalition. "Balance is the crucial thing"—without which one side or another may feel that the planners are promoting a certain position or agenda. For the teen-pregnancy forum, planners have brought in Planned Parenthood, pro-life adoption agencies, the city school board, the Catholic diocese, the Hispanic Coalition, a predominantly African American hospital, and the coordinator for youth services for the county, among many others.

The Common Ground approach is not easy, and its impact and achievements may be modest. It is quiet and grassroots, not flashy and well known. But for the greater good to be true and lasting, it has to be built one brick at a time. Common Ground offers one concrete model for how we might begin building up, instead of tearing down.

JULIE POLTER*

DAY 6 · Putting Faith into Action

The set of issues that come under the broad topic of a "consistent ethic of life" are some of the most contentious in American public life today. In particular, the issue of abortion immediately evokes very strong responses. As writer Amy Sullivan reminds us, "For 30 years, abortion politics has required Americans to choose sides. You are either pro-choice or pro-life. If a politician supports a parental notification law, he or she is labeled pro-life by abortion rights supporters. But if the political leader also opposes a 'partial-birth abortion' ban, the anti-abortion side will tag him or her as unacceptably pro-choice. There is no word for a middle-ground position in American politics."[9] Given the great passion that attends these issues, it would be hard to overstress the importance of factual accuracy. We must educate and speak to the more than two-thirds of Americans who actually fall into the middle ground on this issue, "believing that abortion should be available in some," says Sullivan, "but not all, circumstances."[10] Educational activities are central to moving from slogans to serious solutions on how to reduce the rate of abortion.

Whether or not one agrees with court opinions on abortion, it is worthwhile to examine the factors considered by the courts. And since we have argued that a holistic and consistent ethic of life runs much deeper than simply the abortion issue, it is necessary to engage also in a broader educational exercise—one that covers U.S. and global abortion trends but also addresses poverty, infant and general health care, and the use of the death penalty and its disproportionate punishment of minorities and the poor.

While it is critical to structure educational efforts in a way that expands this discussion into all the areas we have discussed, it is also likely that individuals will choose to specialize in particular issues. A team approach is useful. The methods of activism mentioned in the appendix might be used in a way that allows individuals to focus their own attention while still participating in an overall voice for a broader and more holistic ethic of life. For instance, a letter or opinion piece might be written by an individual with a particular interest in a given topic but then be signed by all members of a group or by a group identity established for this purpose.

---

* *Julie Polter is an associate editor at* Sojourners. *This text appeared in* Sojourners, *Sept./Oct. 1996, vol. 25, no. 5, pp. 10–11.*

There are also many opportunities to participate in demonstrations and acts of nonviolent resistance that bear witness to individual components of a consistent ethic of life. See the appendix for ideas about such possibilities.

DAY 7   Group Meeting and Reflection

1. Develop a one-page statement outlining what you think would be a consistently pro-life political position. Imagine what critiques might be offered by others and integrate those critiques into your response. Keep in mind the various facts and statistics cited throughout this chapter.

2. Discuss the various points of the opinion written by Justice Blackmun in *Roe vs. Wade*.[11]

3. Read Cardinal Bernardin's 1983 speech "A Consistent Ethic of Life: An American-Catholic Dialogue."[12] How would you go about building a biblical case for a consistently pro-life position? What key themes would you integrate into your position?

4. Discuss the underlying causes that give rise to abortion. What sort of proposal to seriously reduce the number of abortions do you think would attract wide support?

5. What arguments would you use if asked to defend the death penalty? To argue for its abolishment? Discuss and critique both positions.

6. How would you characterize your denomination or group's response to the AIDS crisis? If you find it inadequate, what steps should be taken to begin to correct this?

7. Assess the following claim from *God's Politics,* page 79: "Couldn't both pro-life and pro-choice political leaders agree to common ground actions that would actually reduce the abortion rate, rather than continue to use abortion mostly as a political symbol?"

8. *God's Politics* cites Cardinal Bernardin's call for a "seamless garment of life." What does this mean? Would you defend the sort of position this suggests? Why or why not?

9. What other important "life" issues would you include in your "seamless garment"?

Racism

THE ISSUE OF RACISM is a persistent one in American culture. Slavery is no longer a legal economic practice, treaty rights with Native Americans are at least tacitly acknowledged, and equality has been written into our legal systems. But racism is persistent largely due to the fact that the correction of racial prejudice in the laws did not come with restorative justice, nor did it address "institutional racism" in various societal policies and structures or—perhaps most important—the deeply rooted sin of racism in the human heart. In this week's study, we will turn our attention to the issue of racism and its expression in contemporary society. *God's Politics* covers this issue in chapter 19. Read or review that chapter as you work through this section. The following paragraph provides an overview of the material.

    Chapter 19: Telling the truth about race has always been difficult in the United States. We must start by acknowledging that, as I wrote in a *Sojourners* resource, "The United States of America was established as a white society, founded upon genocide of another race and then the enslavement of yet another."[1] I noted that, theologically speaking, racism is America's "original sin." Slavery and the subsequent discrimination against African Americans in the United States is a magnitude of injustice that requires national repentance. And that is also true, in different ways, regarding the multicultural mosaic that makes up twenty-first-century America. If Jesus has broken down every dividing wall between Christians, then Christians must have a united front in battling every kind of discrimination, bias, and racism.

DAY 1   Introducing the Topic

    What exactly is racism? Is there a common definition? And, most important, what are racism's underlying causes?

    The above-mentioned article, titled "America's Original Sin," gets at the heart of the matter. Prejudice may be a universal human sin, but racism is more than an inevitable consequence of human nature or social accident. Rather, racism is a system of oppression for a social purpose—a purpose that is often economic in nature. The equation that results is "Racism equals prejudice plus power."

In the United States, the original purpose of racism was to justify slavery and its enormous economic benefit. The particular form of racism on this continent was inherited from the Spanish, who viewed the indigenous peoples of the Americas as "animals." The English justified their own slave trade with Africa by defining Africans not merely as unfortunate victims of bad circumstances, war, or social dislocation but rather as less than human, as objects, chattel, property to be bought and sold, used and abused.

The high standards set by the Declaration of Independence (all persons endowed by the Creator with inalienable rights, etc.) were not upheld in the early days of the United States. Native Americans were massacred and driven off their lands. Kidnapped Africans were not given any rights but rather were treated as subhuman property.

While slavery has been around for as long as recorded history, it has not always been racially motivated. Slavery has sometimes been the result of economic misfortune, war, or social dislocation. Plato even argued that certain people were fit to be slaves due to their inherent abilities.

Of course, given the economic benefit of free labor, there is never any shortage of people willing to make arguments justifying such racism. Yale Divinity School theologian Miroslav Volf notes that demonization is often used to justify the mistreatment of one group by another.[2] In order to justify unjust tactics pursued for economic reasons, people often make demonizing statements to create a critical moral distance between those in power and those without power. To the church's eternal embarrassment, Christians have too easily become the supporters and theological enablers of racist practices.

In the contemporary period, we dress up our racism in new justifications. Why do we continue to struggle with a racial divide in this country? The popular TV show *ER* once featured an interchange between an African American nurse and a white doctor. When a black gang member was brought into the emergency room with a gunshot wound, the doctor provided treatment, but the youth died. The brother of the dead gang member threatened to sue the doctor for not giving adequate treatment because of racial bias. The doctor then asked the nurse, his friend, "Do you think I gave this patient substandard treatment due to his race?" She responded, "To you folks, it's never about race; but to us, it always is."

Theologian James Perkinson put it this way: "'Race' as definitive of the central relationship organizing social wherewithal and political opportunity in the history of [the United States] yields a structure of white domination and non-white subordination in general, but also a particular paradox of empty passivity on one side of the color line and potent struggle on the other."[3]

Some people think that they have moved beyond racism because some of the most offensive and overt forms of racism are gone. Yet subtle forms continue to survive. The 2005 Academy Award–winning movie *Crash* explores some of the variations and subtleties of race and racism. This provocative film examines the complexities of racial conflict in America, in the context of post–September 11 Los Angeles. The multiethnic cast examines fear, bigotry, and racism from multiple perspectives as a number of lives intersect. Film reviewer Roger Ebert said, "One thing that happens, again and again [in *Crash*], is that people's assumptions prevent them from seeing the actual person standing before them." The dialogue in the film includes many different languages that are often not translated for the viewer into English subtitles on the screen. What feeling does this create in the viewer? How might it illuminate or critique nativist "English-only" movements in the United States? The director, Paul Haggis, makes sure that the film shows various racial and ethnic stereotypes that people hold. But the script plays with these stereotypes, twisting them to show how they are fundamentally false and yet have superficial elements of reality. Consider viewing this film with others and hosting a discussion.

Racism can be very deeply hidden, and it can show up in our interpersonal practices at unexpected times. If we are white, many of us, if candid, can think of times when we have consciously used white privilege to our own advantage. Our entire society is set up to allow our white skin to ease our way. If we are people of color, many of us, if candid, can think of times when we have allowed our bias against those with economic or social power over us to block us from having a more human interaction. Many aspects of our society are set up to put obstacles in the way of people of color. The frustration and bitterness that can build up in response to these obstacles have the potential to eat away at all our souls.

As we work through this week, let us be particularly attuned to our emotional responses, to honestly see where racism or bias is at work within us. It is not possible for whites in America to claim to be "beyond race." If we accept that fact, we can begin to heal and grow toward the person Christ calls us to be. On issues around race and racism—perhaps in even deeper ways than with the other themes we have been discussing—our first step forward is the recognition of our own need for repentance.

DAY 2

Considering the Evidence

In this section, we will consider several statistics about the ways that people of different races are able to access the resources available in our country today. The picture is not a pretty one. The sad but inescapable conclusion is that racism is alive and well in America, and that minorities are suffering the consequences in very concrete ways.

According to the 2000 census, the U.S. population in that year was roughly 75 percent white, 13 percent Latino ("Hispanic," in Census Bureau language), 12 percent African American, 4 percent Asian, and 1 percent Native American.[4] Even using these statistics it is important to remember that Census 2000 saw the first major overhaul of the census questionnaire in forty years. "The big issues for Census 2000 revolved around our social identity crisis—specifically how we define 'race,' 'ethnicity,' and 'culture,'" wrote Rose Marie Berger in her article "Knock, Knock. Who's There?" She noted that "since 1977, people have been required to identify themselves on census forms by choosing only one racial group—black, white, American Indian and Alaskan Native, Asian or Pacific Islander. In 1997, Congress decided *against* adding a single 'multiethnic' category to Census 2000, opting instead to allow multiple checks under 'race.' This increases the racial options from 15 to 32,000 possible combinations."[5]

The census notoriously undercounts minorities. In 1990, racial and ethnic groups, renters, and children were severely undercounted. Asian Pacific Americans were undercounted by 2.3 percent, compared to a 0.8 percent undercount of whites. The undercount rate for Latinos was 5 percent, the highest for any race or ethnic group except American Indians. This is important because census data are used to allocate more than $180 billion of federal funds, to redistrict local, state, and legislative boundaries, to reapportion congressional representatives, and to gather demographic data. The numbers matter.

Using census data, we can compare the median incomes of the major groups—namely, white, Latino, and African American—and see how the incomes have changed between 1972 and 2001.[6] The median income in white households increased from $36,510 in 1972 to $44,517 in 2001. For Latinos in the same time period, median income increased from $27,552 to $33,565. For African Americans, it increased from $21,311 to $29,470.

Note that "economic booms" disproportionately help white households and offer the least for African Americans. Also, while progress is slowly being made, by 2001 both Latinos and African Americans shown in this data fell behind the income levels of whites by as much as a third.

Areas that reveal the extent of racial disparity include poverty levels, incarceration rates, and access to health care. On poverty, we can summarize the data rather quickly. Shown below are poverty rates for 1959, 2000, and 2004. (*Note:* The Census Bureau omits some data—hence the gaps below.)

Poverty Rates

	1959	2000	2004
Blacks	55.1%	22.5%	24.7%
Whites	18.1%	9.5%	10.8%
Latinos	21.5%	21.9%	
Asian	9.8%		
Total	22.4%	11.3%	12.7%

The picture is even more discouraging when you consider the poverty rates among children. In 2004, the poverty rate for African Americans under age eighteen was 33.6 percent, for Latinos it was 28.9 percent, and for whites 14.8 percent.[7]

Incarceration rates are also higher for minorities, and many studies have provided evidence that racial bias is a large part of the reason. One example is the phenomenon commonly known as "DWB" (driving while black). An African American out for an evening drive is more likely to be pulled over by the police than a white driver—for no reason other than race. Likewise, members of minority groups commonly receive more severe prison sentences than white people when found guilty of the same crime. In post–September 11 America, this is especially true of Americans of Middle Eastern descent. According to news reports, in cases involving non-Muslim Americans and corporations charged with violating sanctions against Iraq, the government has asked for warnings or civil penalties, not jail. On the other hand, Americans of Middle Eastern origin convicted of the same charges have been given extremely long jail sentences and high fines.[8]

The incarceration rates for minorities, and for African Americans in particular, are significantly higher than they are for whites. In 2000, whites—who total 75 percent of the general population—made up 35 percent of the prison population. Latinos—who made up 13 percent of the general population—were 18 percent of the prison population. African Americans—who were 12 percent of the general population—made up 44 percent of those in prison. In 2000, the total prison population was comprised of almost two-thirds non-whites, while the general population was more than two-thirds white.[9] According to The Sentencing Project, a nonprofit organization nationally recognized as a source of criminal justice policy analysis, data, and program information: "As the national inmate population has increased in recent decades, the impact of these changes on minority communities has been particularly dramatic. Two-thirds of the people in prison are now racial and ethnic minorities, and for black males in their twenties, one in every eight is in prison or jail on any given day. Moreover, black males born today have a one in three chance of going to prison during their lifetime, compared to a one in seventeen chance for white males. These trends have been exacerbated by the impact of the 'war on drugs,' with three-fourths of all drug offenders being persons of color, far out of proportion to their share of drug users in society."[10] The most glaring example is the disparity between sentencing for possession of crack or powder cocaine. Possessing 5 grams of crack cocaine carries a mandatory minimum penalty of five years, the same as possessing 500 grams of powder cocaine. Approximately two-thirds of those who use crack are white, yet 85 percent of crack defendants are African American. Thirty percent of powder cocaine defendants are African American.[11] While looking at these facts and figures, keep in mind that each statistic represents a man or a woman with loved ones—with spouses, friends, parents, and often children.

What are the reasons for this disparity? Is it a discriminatory justice system? Does poverty create conditions that fuel crime among minorities? Do white privilege and power tilt the playing field against persons of color? Is it a combination of these and other factors? Why are Latinos and African Americans more prone to being charged with crimes, more prone to getting prosecuted—and more prone to having a poor defense?

Perhaps most disturbing of all are the racial disparities in the number of executions and death row inmates. "In 82 percent of the studies [reviewed]," a 1990 U.S. General Accounting Office report on death penalty sentencing revealed, "the race of the victim was found to influence the likelihood of being charged with capital murder or receiving the death penalty, i.e. those who murdered whites were found more likely to be sentenced to death than those who murdered blacks." From 1976 to the present, African Americans convicted of killing white people have been 17 times more likely to be executed than white people convicted of killing African Americans. In October 2005, death row across the country consisted of the following racial distribution: 45.5 percent white, 41.7 percent African American, 10.4 percent Latino, and 2.3 percent "other."[12]

Racial profiling, incarceration rates, and statistics on the death penalty and death row all reveal conclusively that African Americans are disproportionately on the receiving end of harsher treatment in the justice system, and Latinos aren't far behind. Again, why is this the case?

Are we ready to face the demon of racism that still hovers over life in America? Are we ready to put legs on the claim that all are endowed by our Creator with certain inalienable rights, and that equality and justice for all are at the very center of those rights? Until we do, we will not live up to the divine call for our lives.

DAY 3 — Reading the Bible

Any discussion of the Bible and racism should begin with the observation that all persons are created in the image of God and therefore stand before God as equals. The first eleven chapters of Genesis, which track the human decline into sin, remind us that we humans are far from God's intentions for us. God's call to Abraham and Sarah in Genesis 12 reveals the beginning of God's grand rescue mission. Perhaps the Hebrew Bible's greatest step forward in that plan is the Exodus from Egypt and the giving of the law at Sinai. God begins the process of restoration of the wayward creation. The law, then, is first and foremost about establishing who this God is who has taken Israel as a chosen people. God does not intend that the people be misled by the pagan cultures that surround Israel. Within this context, God's call for separation from the surrounding cultures is for purposes of education and binding God's people to the covenant. It is not separation based on race.

"In biblical terms, racism is a demon and an idol.... To be even more specific, it is the idolatry of whiteness, the assumption of white privilege and supremacy, that has yet to be spiritually confronted in America and, especially, in the churches.... We might even inquire into the ancient spiritual practices of exorcising demons when dealing with one so virulent as racism."[13]

Theologian Bill Wylie-Kellermann writes that idolatry might be the main spiritual mechanism by which the divinely created diversity of the human family becomes twisted into "a power of division, a device of injustice, a demonic servant of death."[14] To put it another way, racism is an issue of justification. How does one justify one's faith? In Christ or in worshipping one's power?

The teachings of Jesus—and later of Paul—make it clear that there is no basis for separation and exclusion based on race.

Let's examine the parable of the Good Samaritan in Luke 10:25–37. This parable is answering a question posed by a religious leader seeking to "justify himself" (verse 29). The question is this: Who is my neighbor? It is clear that this religious leader expects an answer that will reinforce his current behavior. What he gets, however, is rather different! Rather than affirm existing patterns, Jesus tells the story of a man who, while traveling between Jerusalem and Jericho, is robbed and left for dead by the side of the road. One by one, religious leaders—models of religious faith—"pass by on the other side," ignoring the man. But a Samaritan, a member of a group of people hated by the religious leaders, not only stops to help but makes longer-term provision for the injured victim as well. In other words, the hero of Jesus's story is a member of a group looked down upon by the people gathered around him. Jesus not only destroys any basis for exclusion, but also no doubt tweaks his hearers by making the one they respect least the hero.

In the New Testament Paul concludes that claims of justification, meaning, and self-worth located in any ideology or institution (indeed, in anything but God's grace alone) ultimately prove bondage to sin and death. Galatians 3:28 affirms that in Christ there is no longer a basis for racial, ethnic, class, or gender distinctions. The dividing wall has been broken down by Jesus. Among those who follow Jesus, there can no longer be such cultural, racial, ethnic, class, or gender divisions. One immediately wonders how the contemporary church is fairing, given the highly segregated nature of weekly worship in the United States. Wylie-Kellermann reminds us that "'whiteness' is itself an ersatz cultural reality, a social artifice without real substance, virtually a fabrication and a falsehood. That a lie should pre-empt and usurp the truth of God's grace is, well, the work of death's power in this world."[15]

To further see the extent to which racism is unacceptable in the life of Christian faith, consider the Acts 10 account of Peter and Cornelius. Cornelius, a Roman centurion, is recognized as a "devout man who fears God," though he is not a Jew. His desire to know God is reflected by his actions, and God honors Cornelius by sending Peter to him. But God also has to prepare Peter, who is still influenced by old ways of seeing non-Jews. When Peter goes to Cornelius, God has prepared the way. When Cornelius tells Peter of his experiences—he was told by an angel to summon Peter so that he could hear the Christian message—Peter is amazed and responds that God shows no partiality among persons. All are in need of restoration to God, all are acceptable who come, and distinctions based on race or anything else are ruled out. Cornelius, who was once outside the family of God, is now welcomed—even though he is not Jewish! As people called to live out God's intentions, we have no basis for excluding those different from us. We reject racism because of our desire to see people as God sees them, not as we might normally see them.

Paul picks up these themes when he discusses the "wall of hostility" identified in Ephesians (2:14). The hostility referred to there is not racism as such but the division between Jew and Gentile that the fledgling church had resolved to overcome in its life and community. The wall, in one sense, was quite literal. Wylie-Kellermann reminds us that there was in the temple a barrier defining and setting off the court of the Gentiles. Gentiles were forbidden on threat of death from entering the interior courts. Paul, as a matter of fact, was accused of transgressing that very wall with a friend (Acts 21:27–36). He was arrested and imprisoned for breaking the segregation laws.

Paul's letter to the Ephesians, written while Paul was in jail, argues that in Jesus's death and resurrection the dividing wall of hostility has been broken down and a new humanity has thereby been created in the One who is our peace. It continues:

> For this reason I, Paul, a prisoner for Christ Jesus on behalf of you Gentiles—assuming that you have heard of the stewardship of God's grace that was given to me for you, how the mystery was made known to me ... that is, how the Gentiles are fellow heirs, members of the same body, and partakers of the promise in Christ Jesus through the gospel.
>
> Of this gospel I was made a minister ... to preach to the Gentiles the unspeakable riches of Christ, and to make all men see what is the plan of the mystery hidden for ages in God who created all things; that through the church the manifold wisdom of God might now be made known to the principalities and powers in the heavenly places. (Ephesians 3:1–10)

Taking the liberating word of Jesus to the Gentiles requires addressing the powers directly and putting the "apartheid" wall on notice.

The gospel of Mark, as scripture scholar Ched Myers has shown, incorporates similar themes.[16] In Mark's gospel Jesus sends the disciples repeatedly over to "the other side" of the "sea." Mark is the first person to call that turbulent Galilean lake a "sea," thereby invoking not only the power of chaos but the whole history of crossing to liberation.

"What could be truer to our own experience of trying to build alliances or friendships or communities with sisters and brothers on the 'other side'?" writes

Wylie-Kellermann. "We hear an invisible whisper that says, 'Stay home,' striking fear in our hearts and prompting our despair. It may be a silent storm within, simply awkward and cool, or one raging with hostility. Once again, that storm, that blustering barrier, must be named and rebuked with authority. It's nothing short of a baptism to set off in faith into those troubled waters."[17]

Finally, perhaps one of the most powerful images relating to ethnic inclusion in all of scripture is Revelation 7:9: "After this I looked, and there was a great multitude that no one could count, from every nation, from all tribes and peoples and languages, standing before the throne and before the Lamb, robed in white, with palm branches in their hands."

What more powerful picture of radical inclusion than this? We should focus our attention on two important points. First, this vision does not include the dissolution of ethnic diversity. Notice that the writer has not lost his ability to distinguish between persons of different ethnic backgrounds. Indeed, he explicitly recognizes that there are persons present from all nations, tribes, and languages. Persons from any and all groups are welcome, and they are united in their adoration of the Lamb who was slain. Second, while those ethnic diversities remain (can we be so bold as to declare them celebrated?), they no longer create division or hostility. All people are now bound together under the aegis of the cross with a deeper bond than could be threatened by differing ethnic backgrounds.

DAY 4 — The Christian Tradition

> I still have a dream … that one day this nation will rise up and live out the true meaning of its creed: "We hold these truths to be self-evident: that all men are created equal." I have a dream that one day on the red hills of Georgia, sons of former slaves and sons of former slave owners will be able to sit down together at the table of brotherhood. I have a dream that one day, even the state of Mississippi, a state, sweltering with the heat of injustice, sweltering with the heat of oppression, will be transformed into an oasis of freedom and justice. I have a dream my four little children will one day live in a nation where they will not be judged by the color of their skin but by the content of their character. I have a dream today.
>
> MARTIN LUTHER KING JR.[18]

The church has a checkered history when it comes to the issue of race relations. One of the low points for white Christianity in America came during the period prior to the Civil War. Much of the church not only turned a blind eye to slavery, a blight on the soul, but often provided biblical arguments in defense of the white majority holding black slaves. We will not repeat here those despicable arguments, but Christians—both white and black—must understand this part of our past if we are to move forward together.

While errors are always easier to see in hindsight, some Christians at the time had the gift of foresight and called the church to a better way. Lecturing on possible hindrances to revival, in 1834 Connecticut preacher Charles Grandison Finney had this to say:

> Revivals are hindered when ministers and churches take wrong ground in regard to any question involving human rights. Take the subject of slavery, for instance. The time was when this subject was not before the public mind. John Newton continued in the slave trade after his conversion. And so had his mind been perverted, and so completely was his conscience seared, in regard to this most nefarious traffic, that the sinfulness of it never occurred to his thoughts until some time after he became a child of God. Had light been poured upon his mind previously to his conversion, he never could have been converted without previously abandoning this sin. And after his conversion, when convinced of its iniquity, he could no longer enjoy the presence of God, without abandoning the sin for ever.[19]

While slavery in the United States has been abolished, can we say that the underlying seeds of racism and prejudice have been eliminated? Given some of the statistics cited above, it would be hard to conclude that as a nation we have outgrown racism. To work to overcome racism in our society, it is instructive to consider the methods used by those who opposed slavery. These methods can be expanded to expose less obvious forms of racism today.

One of the powerful voices against slavery during the late eighteenth and early nineteenth centuries was the English politician William Wilberforce. Interestingly, the last letter written by John Wesley was to Wilberforce. In it, Wesley wrote:

> But if God be for you, who can be against you? Are all of them together stronger than God? O be not weary of well doing! Go on, in the name of God and the power of his might, 'til even American slavery (the vilest that ever saw the sun) shall vanish away before it.
>
> Reading this morning a tract wrote by a poor African, I was particularly struck by that circumstance that a man who has a black skin, being wronged or outraged by a white man, can have no redress; it being a "law" in our colonies that the oath of a black against a white goes for nothing. What villainy is this?[20]

Wilberforce had been converted under Wesley's ministry, and it seems the two shared a great passion to see the injustices of slavery and any other form of prejudice undone. What strategies, then, did Wilberforce employ?[21]

Wilberforce lived from 1759 to 1833 and spent about forty years fighting against slavery in Great Britain. Slavery was deeply embedded in the culture and was viewed by many as an economic necessity—particularly by those who benefited most directly. David Gushee observes sadly that, while Wilberforce was able to change the culture of slavery in Great Britain using political tools, in the United States a civil war was required. A key driver of change was Wilberforce's ability to embed his call in the grid of "moral values." Gushee writes:

> One reason that the abolitionist struggle succeeded in Great Britain was the way that Wilberforce appealed to Christian moral values. He hammered away at the theme that slavery violated the law of God even if it was currently permitted by the law of [humanity]. He appealed to the conscience of a nation that was officially Christian and actually included quite a large number of devout Christians. Slavery, he argued, contradicted the moral values that the entire nation as a whole claimed to embrace. The rights and freedoms of the slave-owning class, he argued, needed to give way to the more fundamental and God-given right to liberty of those they enslaved. It took decades for this message to sink in, but it finally did.
>
> There are many lessons in the dramatic story of slavery's abolition in Great Britain, but here I want to reflect on the way in which religiously grounded moral values were employed in the debate. Wilberforce did not hesitate to make moral appeal based on explicit Christian convictions, both because that was his own passionately held worldview and also because it was the official worldview of the entire nation. Wilberforce, of all people, knew that Great Britain fell grievously short of its supposed beliefs every day, but he still found it quite effective to call the nation back to what it said it believed. When he did, no one could argue on principled grounds that slavery was a good and Christian practice. It was slave owner self-interest against the compelling moral values woven into the fabric of national life, and finally self-interest lost.[22]

Much of Western culture is rooted in the Judeo-Christian heritage. Wilberforce was able to tap into the basic moral and ethical commitments of that heritage and call for repentance from slavery on the basis of those commitments. Today, at a time when racism is not as overt as in slavery, yet still quite present, can we take a page from Wilberforce's playbook? Can we once again call our culture to accountability on the basis of Christian moral values? Or has our culture so lost touch with those values that we can no longer call people to better behavior on this basis?

Perhaps even more powerful than the white abolitionists were the black abolitionists and preachers who led the way out of slavery. In 1829, David Walker, the son of a slave father and a free black mother, also used Christian moral and religious language to make his point, concluding that as a result of the sin of slavery God would punish America:

What nation under heaven, will be able to do any thing with us, unless God gives us up into its hand? But Americans, I declare to you, while you keep us and our children in bondage, and treat us like brutes, to make us support you and your families, we cannot be your friends. You do not look for it do you? Treat us then like [humans], and we will be your friends. And there is not a doubt in my mind, but that the whole of the past will be sunk into oblivion, and we yet, under God, will become a united and happy people. The whites may say it is impossible, but remember that nothing is impossible with God.[23]

Henry Highland Garnet, who had escaped slavery in Maryland, was a Presbyterian minister in New York. In 1843 he delivered a powerful sermon to the National Negro Convention in Buffalo, New York.

The declaration [of independence] was a glorious document. Sages admired it, and the patriotic of every nation reverenced the God-like sentiments which it contained. When the power of government returned to their hands, did they emancipate the slaves? No; they rather added new links to our chains. Were they ignorant of the principles of liberty? Certainly they were not. The sentiments of their revolutionary orators fell in burning eloquence upon their hearts, and with one voice they cried, liberty or death. Oh what a sentence was that! It ran from soul to soul like electric fire, and nerved the arm of thousands to fight in the holy cause of freedom.[24]

In addition to the male abolitionists, we also recall the white female abolitionists like Lucy Stone, who taught fugitive slaves how to read and write; Sarah and Angelina Grimké, who spoke against slavery even though their father was a slave-holder; Abby Kelly, who joined Frederick Douglas on his first speaking tours, and others. And the incredibly courageous black women abolitionists: Maria Miller W. Stewart, who spoke publicly in 1832 on "the cause of God and the cause of freedom"; the Quaker leader Sarah Mapps Douglass; Margaretta Forten, founder of the Philadelphia Female Anti-Slavery Society; Sarah Parker Remond, who preached in the United States and Great Britain on the immorality of slavery; Harriet Tubman, who personally helped about 300 slaves escape to freedom on the Underground Railroad.

Finally, we must remember Sojourner Truth, born Isabella Baumfree into slavery in unspeakable conditions. As her hatred toward her white masters grew, she asked God to help her escape. In a spiritual vision God gave her an escape plan. She walked away from slavery, left her slave ways on the cellar floor, and stepped into freedom. Her new name marked her liberation. At the 1851 Ohio Women's Convention, Sojourner Truth hoisted the male preachers and abolitionists by their own petard.

And how came Jesus into the world? Through God who created him and woman who bore him. Man, where was your part? But the women are coming up, blessed be God, and a few of the men are coming up with them. But man is in a tight place, the poor slave is on him, woman is coming on him, and he is surely between a hawk and a buzzard.[25]

There are a number of ways in which one can build a case for rejecting racial prejudice, including the concept of the common good. As we saw in the previous section, there is no correct reading of the Bible that supports racial discrimination. From a Christian perspective, such discrimination is simply immoral. The abolitionists were right to appeal to Christian moral convictions in the fight against slavery, as was Martin Luther King Jr. in the fight for civil rights. We would do well to do likewise in our own time as we combat the remaining vestiges of racism in all their expressions.

DAY 5 — Living Examples in the Contemporary Church

In addition to the life of the church itself, there are a variety of parachurch ministries that engage in issues related to the themes of *God's Politics*. In the following account, John Potter relates to us the transformative power of his tour through key locales of racism and the civil rights struggle in the South. John's opportunity was facilitated by a ministry on the campus of Chicago's North Park University. As you read his account, from his initial struggle with deciding to participate through the misinformation he had to endure and finally to his return home, imagine the various ways that racism still distorts how we think about so many things.

❧ LOOKING BACK TO MOVE FORWARD

"You won't actually go through with this," I silently told myself as I wrote the note. "This is one of those things you know you should do, but you won't." It was a Sunday night "College Life" worship service at North Park University in Chicago, and a speaker had asked those in attendance to commit to doing something that would be a challenge, then write that act down on a Post-it note. The idea was that whatever we wrote would be something that reflected our desire to live Christ-like lives: necessary, but difficult. It was one of the rare moments in which I can truly say that I felt God's call. I wrote down, "Apply to Sankofa."

The "Sankofa" journey is an annual four-day pilgrimage to the southern U.S. that focuses primarily on black and white relations and stresses personal transformation. As someone brokenhearted, frustrated, and angered by the sinful racial injustice of America's past and present social fabric, I'd been interested in the trip throughout my time in college. But as a shy and self-conscious person, and one for whom close relationships usually aren't formed quickly, I'd generally steered away from such hard-core endeavors, no matter how much I felt I *really should* go. I didn't realize that God would use that Post-it note challenge as a means to keep Sankofa in my mind and on my heart for many months.

What I was beginning to realize around the time that the application process for Sankofa began—and what I would understand much more deeply by the end of the trip—was that for me, a white male at a largely white school and in a society that was often geared toward my profile, whether or not I wanted to "deal" with racism and talk about it on a daily basis was a *choice*. For most minorities—including those at small, predominantly white Christian schools—it is not a choice. For those most affected by systemic, social, and personal racism, the reality of racial injustice is something that *must* be encountered every day.

I was sickened by the fact that I had gotten so used to being comfortable in a society that usually catered to me that I was unwilling to experience others' nearly constant discomfort. I submitted my application and prayed for better knowledge of God's vision for justice, and for Jesus to lead me toward reconciliation.

"Sankofa" is a Swahili word meaning to look back and reclaim the past in order to move forward toward understanding. Those accepted into the trip—about fifty students my year—began to prepare for the journey by participating in three weekly sessions led by Dr. Rupe Simms, North Park's professor of Africana Studies. We examined and discussed African history, African American history, and the civil rights movement—as well as racism and racial injustice in general—through lectures, dialogues, readings, and films. Students were each assigned a partner of the same gender but different ethnicity and encouraged to get to know one another outside of the preparatory classes before the trip. These preliminary classes were honest, difficult, and open to discussion and sharing—but they were nothing compared to actually getting on the bus.

Led by North Park campus ministries director Paul Johnson, we piled on the bus and began our excursion by driving through the night. Our group journeyed to Louisiana, Mississippi, and Tennessee. The core of the experience was communicating with and getting to know better one's partner, and dialogue topics were often given by a leader to discuss in twosomes. The microphone at the front of the bus was periodically opened up to the group at the end of a discussion or after one of the race-related films that the students watched on the bus.

It was at various times uncomfortable, frustrating, exciting, and emotionally trying to have the spirit of honest dialogue and truthful confrontation so nurtured and encouraged. Topics of discussion ranged from personal experiences of overt racism to thoughts on history, as well as systemic and social racial injustice. For those whose ideas of racism are limited to personal attitudes and grudges held against certain ethnicities or direct verbal expressions of racism, the stories of minority students and the facts on systemic racism presented were shocking.

In my experience, many of the white students were defensive and quick to dismiss others' stories of racism as either isolated incidents or coincidences. It can be difficult for white students to reconcile the vast differences between the reality they've experienced throughout life and that of minority students. It became clear to me that what was needed on the trip was for the white students to listen and for the nonwhite students to vent and to teach.

When we reached Louisiana, we paid a visit to Frogmore, a historic, preserved cotton plantation. It was alarming to see the ignorance of the site's tour guides, who spoke of the difference between "good slave masters and bad slave masters"—only the "bad ones" beat or raped their slaves. History was being rewritten and distorted to reflect a twisted "ideal" of the South that never was: slaves happily working away in the fields, singing and having a great time; spacious living quarters and an abundance of only the best food for the slaves; as well as top-notch doctors paying slaves a visit when they got sick. It was an in-your-face confrontation with the blatant racism still very much alive in the United States today.

In Mendenhall, Mississippi, we met with Pastor Timothy Keys, president of the Mendenhall Ministries, founded by well-known Christian activist John Perkins in the 1960s to provide services to and meet the physical and spiritual needs of Mississippians in poverty. Keys spoke openly with our group about issues that we presently face as college students in a city as diverse and segregated as Chicago. It was truly eye-opening to be immersed in the concerns and dialogue of black North Parkers, a group that I had known only on the periphery of my experience at school.

In Jackson, Mississippi, we visited Jackson State University to see an exhibit called *Without Sanctuary: Lynching Photography in America.* It was an extremely difficult point in our trip, one in which the inhuman and hateful history of America and of black and white relations—the history that is brushed over in most white students' education—was put in front of our eyes for us to try to understand.

Our final destination was Memphis for a tour of the Civil Rights Museum. For Americans to move forward in reconciliation it is vital for us to fill ourselves with knowledge of the struggles and victories of the past—especially given the fact that the civil rights movement is still the fairly recent past. What came to mind for me while seeing and hearing the many stories in the museum was that, as *God's Politics* emphasizes, *we* are the ones we've been waiting for. Our proper response to looking back at history and understanding it clearly and accurately is to identify the ways in which the struggles are still apparent today in our immediate surroundings, and to use the knowledge and experience we've gained to push things forward ourselves.

After the museum, we walked in small groups along Beale Street. What I still remember vividly from that relaxed last evening after a weekend of sometimes painful revelation was how strongly I felt a sense of grace—God's grace in redemption and resurrection, that past mistakes and sins can be wiped away with the hope of building the kingdom, but also the grace that my brothers and sisters of color extended to me. We had just spent a weekend focusing on the horrible things white people have done to people of color throughout history and still today, and I was accepted and treated as a friend with no questions asked. What a wonderful example of Jesus's grace toward humanity.

We spoke throughout the journey of an "aha" moment we might experience, in which the whole idea of Sankofa suddenly clicks and works for you—where you see history and its implications for today and suddenly "get" how it all works together and how you can respond. For me, the "aha" moment was realizing that the real journey starts when you get off the bus at the end of the trip. The Sankofa trip is an introduction to a life of seeking reconciliation and right relationships, of working to dismantle racism and injustice in all that one does.

It is a constant challenge to live up to what I took away from this transformative experience, now seeing for myself and understanding more deeply the reality of racism for people with whom I've formed relationships.

JOHN POTTER*

DAY 6 · Putting Faith into Action

Many of the themes that we discuss in this book can be most clearly understood through experiential educational events. This is especially true of racism. One of the great problems that still surrounds the issue of racism is the extent to which white Americans continue to believe that the problem has been solved. They tend to claim that the sorts of things that racial activists point to as evidence of lingering racism are misunderstood. This suggests that our culture at large will be quite resistant to the more common means of education. We may need to get more creative.

One potential tool that can help deepen understanding is drama. The Internet is a good place to find good dramatic pieces that help to focus attention on particular aspects of the problem of racism. If you are part of a larger support group working on race issues, you and your partners might create a dramatic presentation that draws attention to particular racial concerns in your area. As you select dramatic materials, you should consider just how ready your potential audience is to be confronted by these issues. The goal, of course, should be to draw your audience in so that they, too, feel the alienation and dissonance of racism.

Another resource is found in tests aimed at revealing the many privileges that the majority enjoys. An example is the remarkably powerful tool called the privilege test. Everyone lines up on the center line of a basketball court. Participants are told that there is an important prize at the front of the gymnasium and that they are to race for it. Before the race starts, however, there are certain restrictions. If you are a person of color, take one step back; if you were raised by a single parent, take one step back; if you had more than fifty books in your house as a child, take one step forward; if your parents read to you as a child, take one step forward; and so on. The list is quite long. It is also very moving. Participants are often embarrassed to realize how privileged they have been. Others are moved to see how far they have come even with unprivileged childhood experiences. Sometimes, participants are moved to express

---

* John Potter is online giving development assistant at Sojourners/Call to Renewal.

appreciation to parents for the fine job they have done in difficult circumstances. The bottom line is this: all feel the force of the different ways that life experiences, many explicitly tied to racial prejudices, can affect our lives. When planning such an activity, be creative—but keep your focus on the experiential.

Be sure to consider ways in which you can employ many of the different ways of being socially active that are outlined in the appendix. Look for opportunities to engage in letter writing; antiracism and diversity training in church, community centers, and the workplace; or helping your pastor with sermon preparation and the celebration in church of significant dates in the history of racial justice and reconciliation.

DAY 7   Group Meeting and Reflection

1. Discuss the strengths and weaknesses, as well as the implications, of the definition of racism. What is your perception regarding the state of race relations in the U.S. today? What about in your church?

2. What do you make of the high incarceration rates of minorities?

3. The Sunday morning worship hour has been called the most segregated hour in the United States. Why is this so?

4. Do you agree that it is a fact that historical prejudices have created circumstances in which minority groups have less opportunity than the white majority? If so, is this a moral problem? What ought the church to do about it?

5. What are the connections between racism and poverty? What do you know about the history of reparations for slavery? What is the unfinished business of slavery in America?

6. Develop a four-point plan to alleviate the worst abuses of racism still present in the United States.

7. What are the worst expressions of racial prejudice in your neighborhood or city? Where have you gotten your information? What might be done to "lift the mask"?

8. What do you consider to be the primary causes of any racial prejudices you have encountered? To what extent have you encountered racial prejudice in the church or in Christian circles? What rationalizations that empower racist behavior and attitudes do you think people have come to accept?

9. What would it mean, and what would it take, for our society to move toward investing less in the idea of "whiteness" (as opposed to ethnic categories such as Irish or German)? In what ways could this be a genuine step toward racial justice, rather than just multicultural window dressing over continuing inequity? What would such a change mean in your daily life?

Strengthening Family and Community Values

You ARE NEARING the end of your study of *God's Politics*. In the next to last week, we turn our attention to the legitimate concerns that both the political Left and the political Right have regarding the family structure in the United States. Read chapter 20 in connection with this week's study. The following paragraph provides a very brief summary of the chapter's material.

Chapter 20: The concepts of family and community are complex and important ones for Christians. On the one hand, the extended family has been a hub of spiritual and other development back into ancient times. On the other, Jesus calls his followers to a broader sense of family than the narrowly defined, contemporary nuclear family. God calls us into existing communities that certainly include the nuclear family, but also include the extended family, the surrounding community, and the church family. The strength and health of the bonds between family and community are essential to the common good. An explicitly spiritual sense of community needs to be reestablished within our churches, our neighborhoods, and our national politics.

DAY 1 Introducing the Topic

The term "family" is often used as a code word, with too little concrete meaning; it is used to bring to mind a set of related ideas that are not necessarily connected to the idea of family. Instead, it is used to construct a particular way of seeing and connecting an array of issues. For example, when you hear someone speak of "family values," what does it evoke? This phrase has been carefully constructed and used to connote a position that opposes sex education, abortion, gay and lesbian rights, pornography, and "sleazy entertainment." In addition, it often expresses a position that focuses primary attention on the "nuclear family," conceives women first as homemakers, and favors a strongly patriarchal social order.

Now, before we proceed with our analysis, it's important to note that to offer critique of a position as too narrow is not to deny that it has some validity. Too often, critique is taken as wholesale rejection, and we must be more cautious on such serious matters as the health of our families and engage in building common ground wherever possible. This means affirming each side when we can. For example, we will argue that the vision of family values embraced by the political Right leaves out too much. While doing that, however, we can agree that pornography has inundated our society and has coarsened our judgment on sexual matters. We can agree, as *God's Politics* says, that "infidelity, betrayal, broken relationships, and casual sex are undermining the health and integrity of our society" (page 322).

While affirming these points, we must also notice what is missing. When you hear the term "family values," it is rarely connected to the idea of overcoming poverty, which as we have seen is a major threat to family life. It is rarely expressed in a way that makes clear the intimate connection that God intends to exist between families and communities. It particularly fails to recognize that our accountability for others extends well beyond our own immediate families. In fact, one could argue that the Right's version of "family values" encourages individualism. It tends to put forth a very narrow sense of family and community that fails to do justice to the rich sense God intends.

Unfortunately, the ambiguous manner in which the term is used obscures important facts and weakens the public debate. For example, the tendency to use the term "family" primarily in reference to the so-called nuclear family can be misleading. The idea of "family" as nuclear family is a fairly recent construct, only a couple of centuries old. This way of thinking of family makes the term individualistic and private, and it tends to miss the richer sense of family that has been in play through most of the rest of our history.

What does a more biblical concept of family look like? If we examine the Hebrew scriptures, we find the standard notion of family to be much more along the lines of what we call the extended family. There would be a head of the household and his wife, and the sons and their wives and children would live close by. In addition, some displaced persons might also be taken in and become part of the extended family. This provided a much broader, cross-generational concept of family than the contemporary nuclear family. The Bible speaks of extended families of more than a hundred members. We are explicitly told that Abraham's extended family included sixty-six people. While we need not import these details into the contemporary period, reflecting on such models helps us to see the inadequacy of the individualism that is part and parcel of the family values debate. We must begin to think in much broader and communal terms. Our discussion needs to extend beyond the boundaries of the typical "family values" debate if we are to reimagine a more Christian way of being.

To the question, Is the family under attack? we must answer with an emphatic yes. However, the attack is much deeper and more profound than is generally described. First, the family is under attack by discussions that define the term too narrowly. The paradox, of course, is that those doing most of the talking about family values often misdiagnose the problem, making matters worse. Second, the family is under attack on a broad range of fronts including poverty, domestic violence, divorce, missing male parental figures, health-care access, and a consumer-oriented approach to sexuality. The failures of both the political Right and Left are evident here, as *God's Politics* notes (page 326):

> [T]he answer to the "family values" crisis may not be a return to traditional roles for men and women and combating gay marriage, as the Right suggests, but rather in supporting the critical task of parenting—culturally, morally, and economically. Here again, both the Right and the Left are failing us. The Republican definition of family values, which properly stresses moral laxness but ignores the growing economic pressures on all families, simply doesn't go deep enough. Similarly, the Democrats are right when they focus on economic security for working families but wrong when they are reluctant to make moral judgments about the cultural trends and values that are undermining family life.

Both economic factors and broader cultural factors contribute to the dissolution of families. Where do we find hope? The short answer is in building communities that bear more resemblance to biblical notions of family. One good place to start should be the church.

DAY 2 — Considering the Evidence

As we have seen, "family values" have been discussed in the public sphere with a rather narrow sense of family. There are only a limited number of places where one might find communities that embody anything like a deeply biblical view of family.

Data from the 2000 census provide insight into the health of American households. Of the 281.4 million people who lived in the United States in 2000, 273.6 million of them lived in "households," broken down in this way:

Total households	105.5 million
Family households	71.8 million
Married couple heading household	54.5 million
Single mother heading household	12.9 million
Single father heading household	4.4 million
Non-family households	33.7 million
Single person	27.2 million
Multiple persons	6.5 million[1]

Family households are defined as a group where at least one person is related to the householder in some way, including blood relations and adoption relations. Given concerns over the prevalence of divorce, it is worth noting that about 75 percent of those living in households defined as "family households" live in families with married parents. Let's consider some of the other factors indicating the health of these families and see if our analysis can give us a better sense of the ways that the family may be in jeopardy.

Most have heard the claim that somewhere around half of marriages end in divorce. But, as is often the case, the answer you get depends on the question you ask. Perhaps it is more helpful to think about the numbers shown above regarding families that are headed by only one parent and then to consider the number of persons who have been divorced one or more times. Not all such families are headed by a single parent resulting from divorce (some are widows and widowers, for example). It is nevertheless the case that single-parent families, especially families headed by a single mother, are among those most likely to be in poverty or economically disadvantaged.

Let's look now at the percentage of people who have been married and then divorced, from data recently reported by Christian pollster George Barna.[2]

Denomination/Religious Group	Divorced
Nondenominational Protestant	34%
Jewish	30%
Baptist	29%
Born-again Christian	27%
Mainline Protestant	25%
Mormon	24%
Catholic	21%
Lutheran	21%
Atheist/Agnostic	21%

What is striking is the higher divorce rates among the more conservative Christian denominations. Space does not allow examination of the reasons why this might be true, but the issue is a very important one. One last detail on overall U.S. divorce rates: taking all people, religious and not, into account, the U.S. has the highest divorce rate of any country in the world. Again, it would be worth reflecting on why this is so. It adds credence to the following claim from *God's Politics* (page 331):

> To say gay and lesbian people are responsible for the breakdown of the heterosexual family is simply wrong. That breakdown is causing a great social crisis that affects us all, but it is hardly the fault of gays and lesbians. It has very little to do with them and honestly more to do with

heterosexual dysfunction and, yes, "sin." Gay civil and human rights must also be honored, respected, and defended for a society to be good and healthy. It is a question of both justice and compassion. To be both pro-family and pro–gay civil rights could open up some common ground that might take us forward.

Oversimplification of the cultural landscape does not help move us toward solutions, and the lack of stability in marriages, particularly among Christians, suggests that a "remove the log from our own eye first" strategy is appropriate.

The question that has to be addressed is whether poverty is a result or a cause of marital instability. As Christians, our concern for families in general and for the quality of life for children in particular requires us to deal with both alleviating poverty to strengthen families and strengthening families in order to alleviate poverty. In other words, we must take steps to make divorce more rare and two-parent households more common, while also working to overcome stagnant wages, the rising cost of housing and child care, and the negative consequences of "absent parents" in families where low wages require both parents to work.

While there is debate about what is cause and what is symptom, there is no question of a strong correlation between child poverty and the marital status of the household. It is not surprising that when people have jobs they are better able to function as parents—single or married. The highest child poverty rates are among family households with a single mother as the head of the household. In addition to income disparities, access to health care and other similar benefits are least available to children living with single mothers. Thus, *God's Politics* notes, "The legitimacy of the family values debate has been demonstrated in the clear links that have been made between the problem of family breakdown and the social ills of youth delinquency and crime, drug use, teenage pregnancy, welfare dependence, and the alarming disintegration of civic community, especially (but not exclusively) in poor neighborhoods" (page 325).

Most of the discussion here has focused on children in poverty, but our elders are also at risk. Social Security insurance addresses the economic plight that many people find themselves in when they are no longer able to work. To the detriment of the common good, the recent political discussion on Social Security has been almost exclusively focused on privatization. Fifty-seven percent of Americans now say that privatization is a "bad idea," and 71 percent of seniors are "hostile" to the idea.[3] Nevertheless, the only Social Security proposals addressed by Congress include private accounts; they also cut benefits and do not address the coming Social Security shortfall or include steps to extend the program's solvency. "Addressing Social Security requires a moral framework that helps shape prudential judgments about proposals and political leadership," writes Yonce Shelton, national coordinator and policy director of Call to Renewal. "If we want congressional leaders to listen to the people and broaden the debate, we must help them understand what is at stake for *all* Americans, including widows and orphans, the ill and disabled, low-income elderly, and children. We need to put the people—us—back in the conversation, help move the discussion to higher ground, and urge leaders to keep the promise for *all* God's people."[4]

The issue we must work on has to do with replacing our individualistic sense of family with a more communal—and more biblical—concept. We now turn our attention to the family as understood through the biblical lens.

DAY 3   Reading the Bible

Few things are exploited in contemporary politics more than the notion of family. Those on the Right have correctly drawn attention to the importance of the family in building a strong society. Unfortunately, they have so narrowed the concept that it hardly bears resemblance to that rich notion of family that has been in play for most of history. On the other hand, those on the Left have a broader sense of the societal obligations that attend supporting families. Unfortunately, they often miss the importance of the personal aspects emphasized by the Right.

In this chapter, we examine the debates about family that arise in the Bible itself. Earlier, we noted that it would be a mistake to think of the modern nuclear family as adequately representing the nature of family in the Bible. Rather, the biblical model is closer to our concept of an extended family, which might also include adoptees and workers.

In Luke 14, Jesus makes it clear that love of family cannot be the supreme value for his disciples. The allegiance to Jesus and to the kingdom must be so great that we "hate" our families by comparison. This is amplified in Matthew 19 when Jesus affirms that those who have given up the insular security of the family economic system to cast their lot with the poor and serve the kingdom are true disciples. In Mark 3, Jesus has just launched his public campaign and is in trouble not only with the religious leaders (who think he is demon-possessed), but also with his family (who have come to "seize him" because people are saying he's crazy). Jesus separates himself from his family, saying, "Who are my mother and my brothers?" (Mark 3:33) to demonstrate his larger point that "a house divided against itself cannot stand" (Mark 3:25). In other words, the revolution of values that Jesus is calling for will require even a reexamination of "blood ties." "Jesus is remembered by both friend and foe," writes S. Scott Bartchy, a professor of Christian origins and the history of religion at UCLA, "... to have redefined the basis and limits of family life, rejecting blood ties in favor of the faith-based sibling-like bond that he created among his followers. Persons who do God's will have become Jesus' siblings with God alone as their parent (see Mark 3:35, Matthew 12:50, and Luke 8:21)."[5]

There are also relevant examples in Acts and in Paul's letters. In Acts 16, for example, we are told that the entire household of the jailer of Paul and Silas was baptized. Several letters of Paul end with particular greetings to extended families in the area of the church being addressed.

Bartchy has this to say about Paul's interpretation of "family":

> A close reading of Paul's Greek in his letters reveals that he not only knew about Jesus' radical redefinition of "family," but also made it his core relational term to describe the converts in the faith-related, household-based congregations to whom he wrote. Paul profoundly affirmed and implemented Jesus's vision of a society based on the surrogate kinship of faith-related siblings. This shared vision … favor[ed] relationships rooted in the individually chosen and deeply shared commitment to the will of God as revealed by this Jesus. Paul's basic model for his new communities was a family of such "brothers and sisters," without any person in the group, including himself, enjoying the traditional authority and privileges of an earthly parent.

God has created us all to flourish—to be fulfilled by living out the fullness of what God created us to be. Relationship is critical to our living out God's intentions for us. When we ask what form and what role the concept of family has in Christian faith, the short answer is that the family is to be an encouragement to living out the life that God intends. At the center, "family" must be more relational and communal, and less individualistic.

DAY 4 — The Christian Tradition

The early Christians offered a genuinely attractive and distinct alternative to the surrounding cultures. While not always realized in daily life, the early church called for a radical sense of family leadership not based on the Roman patriarchal model (which was itself in flux as women became property owners).

Marriage, as we understand it in the modern sense as "a monogamous, lifetime, romantic union between one man and one woman centered around producing and caring for children," says religious studies professor Ellen T. Armour, "would have been a foreign notion to pre-modern Christians."[6] As we said earlier, the typical Greco-Roman family consisted of a household with wife, husband, children, in-laws, and slaves. The male family head, says Armour, "held life or death power over every member of his household and had sexual access to his wife, his mistresses or lovers, and his slaves." This was the accepted model of most early Christian families and the model Paul is trying to influence.

As the Catholic tradition has emphasized, from the early period on, the importance of the household was so central to the life of the church that the family could be called the "domestic church." Consider, for example, this from Catholic family writers Marie and Brennan Hill:

> The early church began in house churches, where families were the heart of the communities and from which ministers were first called to use their personal gifts to serve the needs of the larger community. The family is the most intimate experience of church, the place where love, forgiveness, and trust should first be encountered. This is the family church, whose members are called to embody Christ in everyday life.[7]

Notice the importance of the concept of "house church." One can easily imagine the development of stronger ties within the local communities as worship happened not only in larger corporate gatherings, but also in the intimacy of each other's homes. We have here an excellent image of both the importance of the extended family unit and the new family of "brothers and sisters in Christ" gathering to worship.

David Balch, professor of New Testament at Texas Christian University, notes:

> For historical perspective it may be worth recalling that in the culture of the early Christians, as important as the family was, it was secondary because Christians' primary commitment was to Christ. This created tensions within the household. At least one effect of early Christianity was to foster a religious perspective that supported some plurality of family systems. For example, women functioned in new ways in early Christian communities—they took on more active, verbal roles. And slaves related to masters in a different way. There was also a reversal in the way that children were perceived: They were seen not just as potential members but as full members of the community—as is suggested by some passages in the gospels, especially in Mark. So there were more family options in a Christian setting than was the case in the broader culture.[8]

One could say that the early Christian movement contributed to the breakdown of the Roman patriarchal family unit. The emphasis of the first Christians was on mutuality in decision making and on empowering one another in ministry based on the gifts of the Holy Spirit. There was not a uniform experience, but the family and community values that Paul emphasizes are those of caring for the least, mutuality, forgiveness, economic sharing, welcoming the stranger, and creating living units that reflect solidarity with the marginalized.

"The definition of household in the early Christian community was in fact very complex," David Balch reminds us:

> You'd have poor people living on the top floor, the wealthy on the ground floor and those of medium income in the basement. In the same house you would have very different economic units. In that kind of structure,

the gospel's idea of the reversal of values has a concrete setting. There was not the kind of zoning we have in modern cities, in which you are able not even to see the poor; you lived in the same houses with them. How to relate to these various people in the household was a primary question for early Christians. There's a lot of literature—especially, for example, in Luke—about caring for the poor in relationship to the household.

At times the church, in its effort to strengthen families, has been unable to properly assess the engines driving damage to the family. The fathers of the early Christian church were ambivalent on a number of things—private property, free markets, charging interest on money. This ambivalence was because they realized in these things the potential for abuse.

"Capitalism undermines traditional social structures and values," writes conservative commentator George F. Will. "It is a relentless engine of change, a revolutionary inflamer of appetites, an enlarger of expectations, a diminisher of patience. It has taken its toll on those values and those institutions that conservatives hold most dear: family farms, local government, traditional craftsmanship, historic homes and buildings."[9]

Unrestrained capitalism appeals centrally to values at odds with the gospel. It is driven by self-interest, but Christians are called to put others' interest ahead of our own. It needs willing, mobile, and committed workers, but Christians have other allegiances and commitments that sometimes stand in the way. For example, children need parents who are present, but advanced capitalism needs workers willing to make the tough sacrifices of time and energy. Too easily, a robust sense of family is the first thing sacrificed on the altar of economic growth.

"It is ironic that the people who want to preserve family values are often the greatest defenders of capitalism," says Mary Stewart Van Leeuwen, a professor at Eastern College. "Now these people would obviously say, 'Oh, well, when we defend capitalism we aren't defending the peddling of pornography.' Well, why not? If you say that the market is to be left to a matter of rational choice among buyers and sellers, without government interference, then why would you make an exception for one kind of transaction?"

In the Christian tradition, the definition of family has changed significantly throughout history. We do well to remember, says Armour, that

> whether to accept divorce and endorse second marriages, for example, was a major issue for the church in the mid–20th century. Yet today, even many conservative protestant churches advertise divorce recovery workshops. Pews in many churches are filled by so-called "blended families." Divorce is no longer a bar to ministry in mainline denominations. Interracial marriages were also highly controversial on religious grounds, yet no major denomination considers race a bar to marriage today.[10]

There have been many forms of family in history. The most common, as we've noted above, is the extended family, where relationships across generations create strong social networks and living arrangements. These extended families and households provide security and stability for all the members, and multiple role models for children as they grow.

How can Christians explore models of family and community today that promote stability and protect the vulnerable?

DAY 5 — Living Examples in the Contemporary Church

There are numerous ways in which our social fabric can be structured to encourage and strengthen families. Living this out in light of God's intentions has implications for both public and private institutions. In what follows, Molly Marsh provides a summary of the family-affirming ministry of a church in downtown Washington, D.C. As we see here, for the church and Christians to argue for a new way of being, we must be willing also to embody it.

❧
"REMEMBER WHOSE YOU ARE"

Shiloh Baptist Church sits squarely on the corner of 9th and P Streets in northwest Washington, D.C., a grand and dignified fixture in the city's Shaw neighborhood—a community that has seen its fair share of unemployment, drug abuse, and skyrocketing housing prices. On a fall Sunday morning, the church is bursting with electricity, its 1,300-seat sanctuary nearly full as several choirs lead the congregation in praise and "hallelujahs." In the sanctuary around them, stained-glass windows, based on tribal patterns of southern Africa, are among the reflections of the church's 142-year history and its beginnings as a congregation of free and enslaved African Americans.

The church, one of the oldest African American congregations in D.C., is biblical in its theology, with a strong sense of mission, hospitality, and service. Rev. Wallace Charles Smith, Shiloh's senior pastor (and a Sojourners board member), reminds worshippers during his sermon to remember whose they are. "Jesus's blood has signed my name," he says. "What is the inscription on your life?" "The Shiloh Spirit," the weekly bulletin supplement, announces the congregation's focus on spiritual disciplines; for the next several months members will read Richard Foster's *Celebration of Discipline* and talk about its themes of inward, outward, and corporate discipleship at the church's Thursday night Bible studies.

When the worship ends, parishioners stream into the Henry C. Gregory III Family Life Center, which sits right next door, for Bible study, meetings (the list printed in the bulletin for this day is two inches long), and after-church fellowship, or to play basketball in the gym upstairs or take a meal at The Tuning Fork, a small diner inside the center. During the week, the center also provides a day-care center, programs for teen mothers, computer and GED classes, and help with food, clothing, and transportation for those who need it. Grief support groups, AIDS programs, affordable meals for senior citizens—some of the church's 4,000 members volunteer with or staff these and many other activities.

The physical structures facilitate the church's three-fold mission, envisioned by Smith and his team of ministers as a "Ministry of Building by Caring"—caring for one's self; for family, friends, and members; and for the community around them. It's a vision that parishioners put flesh to, not just among each other, but throughout the Shaw neighborhood.

MOLLY MARSH*

We have often heard it said, "Give someone a fish and that person eats for a day. Teach someone to fish and that person eats for a lifetime." This is a good explanation as to why faith-based organizations are making a difference in the social service arena. The faith-based service organizations that are most effective are those that teach skills, along with meeting immediate needs.

Traditional methods of social service delivery have often resulted in one-time solutions to recurring problems. Faith-based organizations are often located in the communities they serve and are seen as stable entities by the generally underserved, often ignored populations surrounding them.

In the United States, faith was the motivating factor in the development of many social services. Orphanages, schools, hospitals, and private homes for seniors are just a few examples. This tradition continues today as programs and services to address issues of homelessness, poor or absent health care, educational gaps, hunger, and poverty are sponsored by and delivered through local community-based efforts.

Shiloh Baptist Church's Family Life Center Foundation in Washington, D.C., is an example of an effective organization that strengthens marriages and families and the local community through empowerment, skill development, and advocacy.

Following are eight programs that represent the foundation's work.

The Child Development Center. Established in 1958 as a low-cost day-care and educational development program for preschool children, this center provides academic preparation and instruction uniquely designed to meet the individual needs of each child for physical, social, emotional, and academic development.

The Senior Center for the Deaf and Hard-of-Hearing. This center had its inception in 1982 and offers daily health, educational, and wellness activities for deaf and hard-of-hearing participants. In providing case management,

---

* *Molly Marsh is an associate editor of* Sojourners. *This text appeared in* Sojourners, *Dec. 2005, vol. 34, no. 11, p. 19.*

counseling referrals, and transportation services, the senior center is a magnet for this "special" population.

The Male Youth Project. Since 1982, this program has been transforming the lives of many teenage boys. With a dedicated cadre of committed male mentors, it provides training in literacy, math, science, and computer skills. Through this project boys ages eight to eighteen receive character, ethical, and moral development as well as a strong academic enhancement foundation.

The Shiloh Debutante Program. This program differs from other debutante programs in D.C. because it provides a combination of character, academic, leadership, and spiritual development activities for high school girls. In helping each debutante identify and develop her respective gifts and talents, this program nurtures, inspires, encourages, and enhances academic growth. College scholarships are given annually to high school seniors in the nine-month program.

The Human Services Program. In fulfilling its commitment to assist families whose coping skills are diminishing faster than finite resources, this program provides counseling, emergency funds, transportation, clothing assistance, and referrals to needy adults facing serious crises in their survival endeavors.

The Community Computer Center. With the use of state-of-the-art computers, learners of all ages receive computer training to enhance employability or improve basic skills. Weekend and summer programs are also available.

Church/Community Partners Against HIV/AIDS. This one-of-a-kind program provides outreach, technical assistance, forums, discussion groups, seminars, and workshops to persons infected with or affected by HIV/AIDS as well as those capable of assisting the HIV/AIDS community—including faith-based organizations, beauty and barber shops, nail salons, and community groups.

Teen Mothers Take Charge. More than 200 teen mothers benefit annually from the counseling referrals, social services, and other benefits this holistic program provides. The needs of teen mothers are addressed as the program continues to have success in reducing incidences of pregnancy among unmarried teen girls.[11]

Through these programs, the foundation is able to provide after-school program services, academic enrichment, HIV/AIDS counseling and testing, financial assistance, preschool care, nutrition and health information, interpreting services, social and health-care referral services, and case management. In the end, all are tools for engaging and strengthening families.

DAY 6 | Putting Faith into Action

In a very real sense, many of the issues that we have discussed in earlier chapters also relate to strengthening families and communities. Becoming more politically active will give us an increased level of empowerment to take on the issues that threaten families and local communities. Preventing wars and supporting alternative ways to resolve conflict will contribute to stronger families and communities. In promoting economic justice and poverty reduction, we will defend families and help communities to become more stable and self-sufficient. The embrace of a consistent ethic of life will contribute to a greater sense of the sanctity of life and to the value of each and every person. And given the proportionate damage done to minority families, working to solve racism will help us fortify families and build strong, diverse communities. How could all these actions not help strengthen families?

A huge question in the matter of strengthening families is how we can go about including in our concept of family the biblical concept of extended families along with our nuclear families. This will require a strengthening of the commitment to both, and will require us to begin to see our church family and the broader community as also having a claim on us. This will not be an easy step, and a good deal of patience will be required. However, solid and persistent and repeated education through a variety of channels will begin to change things over time.

In addition to a deeper and richer sense of family, we need for persons on both sides of the political divide to wake up to the valid points being raised by the other side. We must move beyond false dichotomies and sound-bite rebuttals to serious dialogue on what are clear contributors to the many problems that families face. Both economic and sociocultural factors make a difference. We must look for ways to lift families out of poverty, but also look for ways to stem the high divorce rate in America. We must accept responsibility as a society to make sure that working families do not get trapped in poverty due to unjust wage or hiring practices, but we must also work to elevate our attention to the damage done by a society that uses sexual references to sell just about everything. We must realize the importance of good parenting skills, and take the steps necessary to make sure that adequate opportunities exist for all. In other words, we need to come together to put forward a *bipartisan* agenda that deals with *all* these problems.

Work with your local community and neighborhood to figure out ways to educate others and to elicit their perspectives. Build partnerships and use the tools in the appendix to raise awareness on these issues. Since the "family values" debate will be with us for some time, the opportunity will constantly be before you to take proactive steps to get the message out. Most of all, be sure to live that message out daily in your own neighborhoods and churches.

DAY 7 — Group Meeting and Reflection

1. The "nuclear family" is a historically new concept found primarily in highly industrialized Western countries. What concepts of family are represented in the Bible?

2. What do you feel are the greatest pressures on families in the U.S. today? What evidence might you identify to make the point?

3. Why are "extended families" not still the norm in the United States? Are there particular forces that have broken down the extended family? What are they? What might be done about them?

4. What biblical principles do you use when examining the rights and privileges of Christians who are also sexual minorities? Where do you draw your biblical values when it comes to the rite of marriage in the church for same-sex and opposite-sex members? What do you know about the church's history of marriage and commitment between same-sex couples and opposite-sex couples?

5. *God's Politics* discusses the *Survivor* television series. What cultural trends are uncovered by this analysis? What impacts do you think series such as this have on the broader culture?

Hope for the Future

FOR THE LAST seven weeks, we have looked at issues that require the attention of persons of faith. We started with the question of the relationship between faith and politics. From there, we discussed six specific areas of concern—war/peace, economic justice, poverty, a consistent ethic of life, racism, and strengthening families. We hope that in each week's study you have discovered ways in which you, in your local community, can begin to embody that "better way of being" toward which God calls us.

We turn our attention now to the many grounds for hope that stand before us. With every challenge comes opportunity, and with opportunity comes God's empowerment for a better tomorrow. The task before us may not be easy, but radical change rarely comes easily. Join us as we forge ahead toward that better future!

For this week's study, please review chapters 4, 6, and 21 from *God's Politics*. A very brief summary of those chapters follows.

Chapter 4: Constructive criticism is a good thing, in politics as with all else. To be able to see clearly into the current situation and to offer critical analysis is a vital part of participation in the democratic process. However, this process should aim to be more than just a "politics of complaint" that identifies problems but offers no insights as to what might constitute a better way. Protest should point toward that better way through a vision that involves personal and social transformation and the presentation of solutions. Being "for" an alternative brings positive energy and opens new possibilities in the political debate that focusing only on criticism does not. In short, protest is a good and important thing, but the offering of alternatives is an even more powerful contribution to the political dialogue.

Chapter 6: There are three dominant political options in America. One is conservative on everything—from cultural and family concerns to economic and foreign policy issues. The second is liberal on everything across the same spectrum. The third is libertarian—liberal on cultural/family issues and conservative on fiscal/economic policy. A fourth option is profoundly needed on the American political scene—traditional or conservative on issues of family values and sexual integrity, for example, while progressive or populist on issues of economic justice and peacemaking. Now, as some people are beginning to recognize the false dichotomy in seeing everything as either liberal or conservative, Christians have an opportunity to lead a significant change in the political landscape of this country.

Chapter 21: Prophetic faith does not see the primary battle as the struggle between belief and secularism. The real struggle of our times is the fundamental choice between cynicism and hope. Will we be lost in a hopelessness engendered by the daily recounting of various failures? Or will we be empowered by a dream for a better tomorrow? The decision for hope is based upon what we believe at the deepest level of our being—what we hold as our most basic convictions regarding the world and our dreams for the future. In the midst of the failures, there are always little signs of a better tomorrow—a better tomorrow that should be embraced and encouraged by all who follow the Risen One.

DAY 1 — Introducing the Topic

What constitutes "hope for a better tomorrow"? The last chapter of *God's Politics* begins with two citations, one from Isaiah and one from Revelation:

> Do not remember the former things, or consider the things of old. I am about to do a new thing: now it springs forth, do you not perceive it? (Isaiah 43:18–19)

> And the one who was seated on the throne said, "See, I am making all things new." (Revelation 21:5)

These verses are pregnant with hope. *The Chronicles of Narnia* by C. S. Lewis frequently foreshadow a new and exciting turn of events by noting that "Aslan is on the move." In other words, the Christ figure in the novels is no longer in the background, but is moving out to take a place of action. In the above-quoted biblical passages and in the Lewis novels, we see a similar notion—God is on the move, already planting the seeds that will spring forth in something so fresh and good that, in each case, it can only be characterized as a "new thing" that God is moving us toward.

Frequently the writers of biblical narratives relate what seems like a hopeless situation, one that seems to provide no basis for expecting, or even grasping for, a new and better tomorrow. Yet time and time again, after the writers lay out for us the difficult circumstances, they continue the narrative with two hopeful words, "but God …" Things might look really bad, there may seem to be little or no basis for hope, *but God* is on the move and about to do a "new thing." When the Israelites lived in Egypt, Pharaoh made slaves of them and worked them mercilessly. But in the midst of their anguish, God heard their cry and moved to deliver them by preparing, calling, and sending Moses to lead his people out of Egypt to a new and better place. Even earlier, when Abraham and Sarah grew too old, so they thought, to have children, Abraham began to make plans for an heir that was not his blood descendant. But God remembered his promise, and Sarah, though old, bore Isaac. Yes, sometimes hope seems almost extinguished—but God is not finished.

As noted in *God's Politics,* the most serious temptation that Christians face is the temptation to lose heart, to give up hope, and to surrender to the despair of the moment. When this happens, cynicism is often the result. Despair, cynicism, and then acquiescence and acceptance of the state of hopelessness as the status quo mark the descent into an inability to imagine a better future or to strive toward one. As Christians, we must never forget that the hour may be dark, *but God* is on the move already. Can we perceive it? (Before we proceed, go back to *God's Politics* and reread pages 347 to 351, and reflect on how the power of belief that a new future was possible enabled the overcoming of evil.)

Perhaps the first step toward a new tomorrow is the ability to name the present darkness. Often we find ourselves inundated with a sense of confusion, a vague awareness that something is not quite right, but without being able to name the source of these feelings. Right now, there are numerous reasons for discouragement. We are engaged in a disastrous war in Iraq that was not wisely undertaken; economically, the playing field has been shifted to favor those already well-to-do and to harm those already on the margins; political discourse is rancorous, and bipartisanship seems merely a vestige of the past; and, perhaps most sadly, we find that the loudest voices coming from the "church" often seem more opposed to than supportive of the gospel of Jesus. There are many reasons to be discouraged; there is much temptation to fall into despair and cynicism. Might it be the case that, even in the midst of all this, God is already on the move?

Those on both the Right and the Left who name current circumstances as fundamentally a spiritual failure are, we think, largely correct. Our culture, even the Christian aspects of our culture, has repeated an error often recorded in scripture—namely, becoming immersed in idolatry, an idolatry that makes our comfort more important than our obligations to care for those less fortunate. Israel often fell into the idolatry of nationalism, the tendency to see God's call as first and foremost about receiving a blessing, and failed to see that they were to be recipients of a blessing *in order to be a blessing to others.*

Once the first step toward unleashing "hope for a better tomorrow"—naming the problem—has been tackled, we then begin to envision the nature of that better tomorrow. Recall the passage from the Hebrew Bible, "Without vision the people perish."

A vision for a better future includes a realization that being created in the image of God means being created first and foremost for relationships of self-giving love. It means reaffirming the biblical call to self-denial for the sake of others and a willingness to fight both injustice and expressions of Christian faith that enable and empower the continuation of injustice. It involves repentance for past failures and a concrete and specific determination to embody, at every level, God's intentions for how our shared lives are to be structured. The Christian vision, in its most basic form, means learning to imitate Christ in his giving of himself for all those whose lives he touched.

When asked the greatest commandment, Jesus gave an answer that tied love of God and love of neighbor closely together. He said that we are to love God with every fiber of our being and that we are to love our neighbors as ourselves. In fact, the way the commandment is worded suggests that one simply cannot do one component without the other. This is the vision that drives hope for a better future: a hope that we can recover the communal orientation of the life that pleases God, in spite of the contemporary popularity of "independence" and "autonomy."

The basis for hope must rest, then, on our ability to name the problem, to envision or to imagine a better way, and then to embody that better way—each of us in our own little corner of the world. Take time to review the epilogue of *God's Politics*, "We Are the Ones We've Been Waiting For," and its appendix. We name there several individual instances of folks seemingly raised up by God to wage change in their spheres of influence. As the Sojourners/Call to Renewal team travels across the U.S. and in other countries, we are seeing a consistent and growing dissatisfaction with the current state of affairs—dissatisfaction bold enough to attract and to empower a whole new generation of persons passionate about living out Christian faith in every nook and cranny of human existence. From Maine to California, from Florida to Washington state, God is on the move, raising voices clamoring for change.

Will that movement achieve the critical mass necessary to formulate and bring into reality the Christian vision for a better, more just way of being? It will if and only if each of us decides that, as *God's Politics* puts it, we are going to bring about a change in the wind, a change in the popular expression of the will of the people. No politicians can resist such a wind change, no administration can overlook it, and we are the ones to bring it about. God is already on the move, bringing that "new thing" into being. The question is, as Archbishop Desmond Tutu once asked a group of seminarians about to be ordained: "Are you ready to join with God?" Are we ready, or will we succumb to our doubts, fears, and cynicism? We are betting the future on the belief that the former is the case. Let us together, hand in hand, become God's partners in realizing that new and better future!

DAY 2 — Considering the Evidence

Once, not too long ago, a chapel service at a Christian college in the United States went on for more than a week, 24/7. The effects of this week of intense reflection, repentance, and renewal would spill out beyond that particular campus for weeks and months afterward. Some say the effects are still being felt in certain circles. Nothing in particular led anyone to think, in advance of the service, that all heaven was about to break loose. The chapel speaker for the day only gave a brief testimony and invited prayer and reflection—what followed was completely unexpected.

One of the leaders of this college was out of town and had to be advised of the "revival" by telephone. He confessed that his absence was a good thing, for if he had been in town he almost certainly would have stopped what was going on. Why? Not because he was opposed in any way whatsoever to spiritual renewal, but rather because he would have doubted that this particular form was a genuine spiritual awakening.

This is worth reflecting on at some length. Here a person in leadership of an explicitly Christian college readily admits he might have squelched a move of the Spirit on his campus if he had had the opportunity—a move of the Spirit that, in retrospect, has been judged quite significant. What do we learn from this story? Well, first and foremost, we learn that the Spirit of God is radically free to bring about renewal in many different forms—and not necessarily the form we expect. Consequently, we must exercise due caution in our evaluation of "movements of the Spirit," paying far less attention to particular forms than to the fruits of the movement. Who knows what God might do and how it might be done? As we pray and work for reawakening to the gospel in our day, let us also pray for eyes to see what God is doing.

Without becoming prescriptive about the form that a move of the Spirit might take, we can consider what elements might be present. How might one characterize a new awakening? What might fuel it? What might stand as obstacles?

The term "Great Awakening" is generally used to describe periods of intense religious fervor that have occurred two or three times in U.S. history. Four conditions of these "awakenings" can be identified:

1. During these periods of intense change, as in all times of change, tensions that existed between the "old" and "new" ways of being created a good deal of anxiety. Whether in the past or today, such tensions often invite reflection on deeper things, which find their root in spirituality. In other words, an uncertain social climate calls us back to our spiritual roots.
2. Prior to past awakenings in the United States, there was a breakdown of community. One of the early awakenings was preceded by the move from the more dense urban areas of Europe to the more widely spread frontier settlements of the "new" world. Community bonds were stretched and snapped, largely replaced with a frontier spirit characterized by radical individualism. This emphasis on individualism increased the stress faced by many on the frontier. Of course, the many inherent dangers of frontier life contributed, but the lack of the community relationships that God has intended for us was also a major factor.
3. This environment invited, or perhaps demanded, a high degree of autonomy and independence if one were to survive. Opportunities for engagement with others in developing lives of active discipleship became increasingly difficult,

and a corresponding loss of respect for authority followed. In particular, church authority waned, and by the third generation, many on the frontier were outside any meaningful interaction with the life of the church.

4. The relevant writings of the period expressed concern with what we would call a decline in piety. In short, neither the corporate nor the personal lives of most people at the time were perceived to be particularly well aligned with God's intent, and awareness of the breakdown was growing.

All four conditions set the stage for openness to spiritual renewal. Our contemporary circumstances are not identical, but we can ask ourselves what conditions we experience that might give rise to similar problems and relational breakdowns.

The first Great Awakening of spiritual renewal in the new world came in the early 1700s. The outcomes of this spiritual awakening included the following:

1. There was an obvious and significant elevation of the importance of the religious life for each and every person. Lives of personal piety once again flourished.

2. Renewed appreciation for the Christian faith resulted, but it was for a faith that tended to be somewhat less doctrinaire than previously. A common, overarching Christian faith developed that still left a good deal of room for disagreement.

3. There was an elevated concern for education. During this period, many great institutions of learning were established, and there was a commitment to make education widely available.

4. There was a move to a concept of salvation that involved not only God's saving action but also the human response, which raised awareness of our own responsibility for our relationship with God and with others.

5. There was a renewed vigor to deal with the social ills that faced everyone.

6. A tendency toward theocracy gave way to a more democratic understanding of human self-governance.[1]

Before we ask what we might do to foster such a new movement of the Spirit in our time, let's turn our attention to the biblical witness to see what insights we might gain there.

DAY 3 — Reading the Bible

As mentioned before, the last chapter in *God's Politics,* "The Critical Choice," opens with two Bible passages (Isaiah 43:18–19 and Revelation 21:5). Our hope, as Christians, lies in the "new thing" that those passages refer to—a new thing that God is doing. It is not just a new thing that we must wait until the end to see. Rather, the new thing we look forward to has already arrived in the life, death, and resurrection of Jesus. In that radical change lies our hope—a hope that has already entered the world, but that must be realized again in each and every generation. Hope can be ignored, but it is there to be tapped into whenever we are willing to be used by God to realize once again that "new thing" (or, to put it another way, whenever we allow "new creation" to break in).

"Hope" in scripture is usually connected in some way to God. "Our soul waits for the Lord; God is our help and shield" (Psalm 33:20) is but one example of how biblical writers assert that the trustworthy basis for hope is God. Many times, however, we allow ourselves to misplace our hope. We think that a better future lies in material success or in gaining power over our destiny in some way. Of course, the perception that we have power over our destiny is little more than an illusion, as the parable of the barns in Luke 12 reminds us. Here, the owner of a farm finds himself with more harvest than he can store. He decides to build bigger storehouses in order to guarantee his future security. However, he does not live out the night; his confidence in his ability to make himself secure was baseless.

Some have argued that human existence is a crushing reality without hope. When things are going well, we do not give much thought to the future. We rightly are taken up in the moment. Yet these experiences do not last forever, and we come to times when our own sinfulness or that of others comes crushing in upon us. Our desire is for escape. How can we bear up under the pressure of estrangement from each other and from God? To hope, then, is to look forward to a time when what seems like the impossibility of the present can be put behind us as we enter a new day. But how does the Bible characterize that "new day"?

The best context is the gospel of John's presentation of the morning of the resurrection. There are striking similarities between the language of John 20 and the language of Genesis 1. The morning of the resurrection is referred to as the morning of the first day of the week. The women come to a place characterized as a garden. They come expecting to find a death and the disordering of life that follows from death. Instead, when they get there they find that the light has overcome the darkness and that life has sprung forth from the midst of death. John tells us that new creation has broken out, and that this new creation surpasses the old. After all, the curse that had wrought havoc in the world has now been overcome in Jesus's giving of himself. The words of the One at the tomb are a powerful expression of hope: "Why do you look for the living among the dead?" There is no greater hope than to find life in the place where we expect to find death!

God bringing life from death is a common biblical theme. At the initial creation of the world, the Spirit of God moves over a lifeless and formless void. Yet, from this, God brings forth all manner of life, from the least creature to the ones who will bear God's own image in the world. God's plan to redeem the world and restore it to right relationship begins with the call of Abraham and God's promise to him that he will become the father of a great nation. As time passes, however, Abraham begins to wonder how God is going to pull this off. He and Sarah, his wife, are getting too old for children. Once again, though, God calls forth life from death—in this case, a child from a barren and "dead" womb.

When God calls the Hebrews as a chosen people, it is not because of their inherent goodness or greatness, but rather because of their "smallness." From "no people," God calls forth and creates a people. In both the Old Testament and the New, the lesson of God's calling life from death is occasionally brought home with the ultimate object lesson: the raising back to life of one who is dead. The resurrection was the supreme act whereby God called life from death. Peter, speaking of the church, uses similar language to describe the call of Israel. Peter says that we were not a people, but God has called us together and, as a consequence, we are now a people indeed.

In addition to God's calling life from death, we can also identify some of the expectations that attend new creation. The prophets tell us, for example, that God will pour out the Spirit on people so that they might bear witness to all that God is doing. In Deuteronomy, we are given a picture of life lived out in accord with God's purposes, characterized by freedom from oppression and the absence of poverty. When Jesus lays out his kingdom vision in Luke 4, it includes freedom from oppression, good news for the poor, and sight to the blind. In Acts 2, we are given a picture of life lived out in the reality of new creation and characterized by the complete and total sharing of goods and life among believers. New creation and good news are but two aspects of the same reality—new creation *is* good news, for it carries with it a hope for human flourishing that cannot exist apart from it.

Look around and reflect on the evil and wrongdoing you find in the world. Do you see oppression, hunger (both physical and spiritual), injustice, prejudice, hostility, and struggling families? If so, fear not, for the promise of new creation is already here. If we overlook this glorious reality, we empower the forces of darkness to limit the expressions of new creation.

Let us not be bound by imaginations that are unable to peer into the darkness and see buds of fresh life and possibility waiting to be summoned forth. Rather, let us be awakened and filled with the Spirit; let us put on the armor of God. New creation is here, and we are agents of that new creation. If we may stretch the metaphor, we are secret agents of new creation—agents sent out by God to sow the seeds that will burst forth in that better tomorrow for which we all long. Before going on to the next section, read again chapter 21 of *God's Politics* and let us covenant together: *We will, with God's help, be agents of new creation.*

The Christian Tradition

In every generation, Christians have embodied hope for the future, though that hope has often taken very different forms. For many of us who grew up in conservative churches, the tendency was to see the world as "going badly." Our only hope was that the long-anticipated return of Christ was just around the corner. Even if things *appeared* to be going badly, the longer-term battle had been won by God in Christ. Whatever the current state of things, we could "grit our teeth" and hang on, since the return of Jesus was just around the bend.

One of the interesting things about church history is that in every generation some have had this same belief, and with great confidence. Each generation could point to evidence in contemporary situations that was believed to be fulfilling prophecy. As one might expect, given the Bible's use of phrasing involving the "millennium," perhaps in no period were people so sure of the impending end of the world as in the late 900s. Obviously these hopes for the immediate return of Christ have been wrong so far.

However, we ought to be careful not to draw improper conclusions from this. God is indeed leading creation somewhere. More specifically, God is leading creation toward a day when, at last, things will conform to the divine intent. Such a hope dominates Christian faith throughout the church's history. Without getting into the particular theories about the end of this age, perhaps the two most helpful passages (or sets of passages) are located in the New Testament. The first is from the fourteenth chapter of John's gospel. Here, Jesus speaks of the coming day when all his followers across time will live together in the presence of God—in God's "house." The second passage is from the latter part of the book of Revelation. Although interpretations of this book are disputed, we can agree that the image of the heavenly banquet draws our attention and our sense of hope. Whatever interpretation we have of all this, hope for the future has been a consistent part of Christian faith.

In addition to the sort of hope that comes from anticipation of the kingdom of God, different movements within the church have placed hope in human activism. In fact, the church has conceived of hope in two primary ways. One group has tended to favor quietism, withdrawing from engagement in social change and simply awaiting God's intervention. The other group has tended to favor activism, focusing its efforts on driving societies to change; this group has been more likely to think they were charged to lead creation to the kingdom. On one hand, one could see how both of these movements have been mistaken. But one could also see them as correct in other ways.

In reality, Christian faith calls us to a way of being that involves both approaches. It has been described as "praying as if all depends on God and acting as if all depends on us." A robust activism that arises out of a deep confidence in God's goodness, love, and faithfulness: these are essential elements of the hope we are to have. Faithful Christian activism is always rooted in the deep understanding that it is ultimately the outpouring of God's grace that brings salvation, and that our actions for justice and peace in this world grow out of that saving grace and are empowered by it, but do not replace it.

Wherever an overly pessimistic view of the future is present, hope suffers. Circumstances can become so overwhelming that we can no longer see a way forward. When this happens, it is easy either to surrender to hopelessness or to give up on our own ability to contribute to improving those circumstances. One has to wonder, though, what it is that causes us to give up our hope and to despair. We are all familiar with the biblical injunction not to fear, and we are reminded that as we love better, we will fear less. Is it not fear, of one thing or another, that squelches our hope? And, in the end, isn't fear mostly a loss of faith?

Our task, as followers of the One who was dead and is alive again, is to be agents of hope in all that we do. To get a glimpse of why hope ought to characterize the way we view the future, take a moment to review each week's Day 5 reflection from this study. Each case includes examples of hopeful disciples who realize that their hope is ultimately in God but simultaneously act as if God's hope is worked out through them. "Pray as if all depends on God; live and act as if all depends on you!"

DAY 5 — Living Examples in the Contemporary Church

There is a very real sense in which the actions that we have listed in the contemporary church in each of the other Day 5 sections are examples of hope in the contemporary church. Weeks 1 and 2 outlined hope for a better way of understanding the relationship between faith and politics and hope for a future in which the church more effectively bears witness to the Prince of Peace. In Week 3, we looked at ways in which the contemporary church seeks to make a difference on matters of economic justice. Weeks 4, 5, 6, and 7 dealt with the church's attempt to create a better future in the areas of poverty, defense of life, racism, and strengthening families.

Take a few minutes to read again those earlier vignettes. This week, be prepared to discuss how each embodies hope and how churches in your local area might begin to effect change in these areas.

Let's return to chapter 21 of *God's Politics* and look for the vignettes embedded in that presentation. Prepare to discuss these as well. In particular, select at least one of them to focus on during your time of discussion for the week. If possible, let each member of the group have ten minutes or so to make a presentation on the one that each finds most significant. Some members of the group may have their own story to tell about how a church or parachurch group they've been involved with has attempted to live out a prophetic hope for a better day. Encourage them to share that story with the rest of the group.

After working through these discussions, talk about your own perception of churches in your area as beacons of hope for the future. A movement to actualize a better day will require a whole host of churches and persons. The challenge will be to create an environment of hope coupled with a sense of faithfulness to and dependence upon God's guidance for us. Balancing the two is not easy, but it is necessary. Also, reflect on the extent to which the old paradigms of "liberal on everything" or "conservative on everything" have broken down. Many who are progressive politically are conservative to middle-of-the-road on many theological issues. As *God's Politics* suggests, the development of a "fourth option" that draws from the prophetic religious tradition to combine the strengths of both sides could be a real source of hope.

This new politics is "traditional" or "conservative" on issues of family values, sexual integrity, and personal responsibility, while being very "progressive," "populist," or even "radical" on issues like poverty and racial justice. It affirms good stewardship of the earth and its resources, supports gender equality, and is more internationally minded than nationalist—looking first to peacemaking and conflict resolution when it comes to foreign policy questions. The people it appeals to (many religious, but others not) are very strong on issues like marriage, raising kids, and individual ethics, but without being "rightwing," reactionary, or mean-spirited, and without scapegoating any group of people, like homosexuals. These people can be pro-life, pro-family, and pro-feminist, all at the same time. They think issues of "moral character" are very important, both in a politician's personal life, and in his or her policy choices. Yet they are decidedly pro-poor and pro–racial reconciliation, they are critical of purely military solutions, and they are defenders of the environment.

Prophetic politics—the new politics toward which we're working—would not be an endless argument between personal and social responsibility, but a weaving of the two together in search of the common good. The current options are deadlocked. Prophetic politics wouldn't assign all the answers to the government, the market, or the churches and charities; rather, it would patiently and creatively forge new civic partnerships where all individuals do their share and everybody does what they do best. Prophetic politics wouldn't debate whether our strategies should be cultural, political, or economic, but would show how they must be all three, led by a moral compass. It is a vision that would find new agreements and new common ground solutions on the issues affecting our country.

You will notice that we've left the next two pages blank. Over the course of the next few months, engage in your own "ministry of hope." Then use these pages to customize your copy of *Living God's Politics* to include your story of how you are embodying hope for a deeper realization of the kingdom of God.

My "ministry of hope"

DAY 6 — Putting Faith into Action

Nothing is more powerful in social activism than embodying a confidence that the best is yet ahead of us. We have discussed many issues in the course of this book, and all can be seen in two ways: as threats and challenges or as exciting opportunities to help in creating that better tomorrow. By becoming socially active in the ways mentioned in previous Day 6 sections, you testify to all those around you, indeed to the entire world, that you have not lost hope and that while you might recognize the challenge and the impinging darkness, you have decided to be an agent of the light. Every time you engage in one of those activities that we have identified as "living God's politics," remind yourself that you have chosen to take the path of hope and be a part of the solution rather than a part of the problem.

What specific things can you do to integrate your activism into an overall message of hope? First, make sure that your educational events are aimed both to convict and to inspire. Don't pull any punches when it comes to identifying problems and their severity. But, at the same time, nurture a budding optimism that the light is dawning and that your audience can sign on to help bring the light to the rest of the world. Likewise, when you engage in a dramatic presentation, be sure that the identification of the problems is tempered with optimism and hope. Do not leave your audience broken and disenchanted with the future.

Second, in writing letters and opinion pieces, whenever possible offer a vision for the future. It is far too easy to become mired in the politics of complaint, and there is surely much to complain about. However, do not forego opportunities to offer better ideas for tomorrow. Be on the lookout for things to affirm, things that offer hope for tomorrow, and then use your letter- and opinion-writing skills to rally the hope of others.

Finally, surround yourself with friends, and be there for each other. Bear each other's disappointments and encourage each other. Rarely will everyone in a group be discouraged at the same time. This helps guarantee that even on the darkest days someone will be able to see the silver lining.

DAY 7 — Group Meeting and Reflection

1. "The biblical prophets were never just complaining; they were imagining a newer world." *God's Politics* (page 47) puts this in the context of offering proposals rather than simply raising objections. What steps would you take to prevent efforts to forge a better tomorrow from being hijacked by complaining?

2. Pick one of the books of the prophets (such as Amos, Joel, or Micah) and read through it quickly. How would you characterize the prophets' criticism as well as their constructive proposals?

3. Reflect on the notion of prophecy as "articulating moral truth." Does this concept offer guidance to how Christians might engage politics? What strengths and weaknesses might be inherent in this approach?

4. *God's Politics* outlines three major political options and argues for a fourth. These are: (1) conservative on everything, (2) liberal on everything, (3) libertarian, which is liberal on social issues and conservative on fiscal issues, and (4) conservative on most social issues and liberal on most fiscal/economic issues. Would this option provide a more consistent biblical position? Why or why not?

5. In a recent op-ed piece, one well-known writer objected to the hard "liberal" vs. "conservative" distinctions. This writer went on to observe that few folks are genuinely either conservative or liberal on all the issues. How might we begin to restore some dignity to the dialogue by moving away from these easy categories?

6. What do you make of the popular claim that "secular humanists" are the underlying threat to our culture? First, how would you identify "secular humanists"? Second, what positions would you expect them to hold? Finally, how would those positions threaten the culture in general and Christian faith in particular?

7. How would you characterize "hope," and how does this concept play a role in our daily lives and daily decision making?

8. Discuss the various examples of hope in this chapter. Which one(s) do you think best make the point? Why?

9. Review the predictions on pages 368 to 372 of *God's Politics*. What three would you choose to invest yourself in realizing? Why? What concrete steps would you take?

A Summary of Social Activism Techniques

JUST ADD CONSCIOUSNESS: A GUIDE TO SOCIAL ACTIVISM

By Liz Carty, Jane Fleming, and Stephanie Seidel

CONTENTS

CONDUCT A LETTER-WRITING CAMPAIGN
MEET WITH YOUR MEMBER OF CONGRESS
CARRY OUT A PHONE-CALLING CAMPAIGN
TIME YOUR MESSAGE
USE THE MEDIA
ORGANIZE A TEACH-IN
COORDINATE A DEMONSTRATION
TAKE CREATIVE ACTION
INITIATE CYBER-ACTIVISM
FINANCE YOUR ACTIVIST PROJECTS
GET THE WORD OUT

This appendix[1] focuses on activism opportunities for students, but all of the ideas can be applied among a wide range of age groups, issues, and organizations. With a little tweaking, you can make any of the following suggestions succeed for *your* group!

CONDUCT A LETTER-WRITING CAMPAIGN

It takes only a piece of paper and a pen to be an effective advocate. People often ask, "Will my letter make a difference?" Yes, it will! Congressional staff members say all it takes is ten to twenty handwritten letters to draw their attention to an issue.

Since writing a letter takes only a few minutes and requires limited supplies, it is the perfect advocacy tool to take anywhere on campus or in your community. Write letters at a group meeting, after class, or at a related event. National, state, and local organizations that follow the issues you care about can provide helpful information, such as sample letters and fact sheets. Also, check out the Cyber-Activism section of this guide for information on how to effectively use email to communicate with legislators.

If you're an active young person, you can write to the representatives of your school's district and state, or of your hometown. Check out the Web sites listed in the reference section below to find your members of Congress by zip code. If you're hosting a campus-wide letter-writing table, don't worry about knowing the address of each member of Congress. Students can always write to the representative and senators from their school's district and state.

For more targeted letters, write to your representatives who are on key committees. Web sites—including the ones listed in the reference section below—and congressional guides in public libraries list the committees each member of Congress serves on and explain what the committees represent. Don't be tempted to write to a key representative to whom you have no connections. Many congressional offices disregard mail that is not from a student or constituent in the district or state.

Most congressional offices respond to handwritten letters with information about their positions on the issue. If your elected official is not supportive, find answers to his or her concerns. If your representative takes your recommended action, write a thank-you note. It shows you care enough to watch how your representative responds. Be sure to stay in touch with that person throughout the year, track the progress of your issue in Congress, and let your representative know you voted on election day!

Important contact information:

Representative _____
U.S. House of Representatives
Washington, D.C. 20515

Senator _____
U.S. Senate
Washington, D.C. 20510

Capitol Switchboard: (202) 224-3121

President _____
The White House
1600 Pennsylvania Avenue NW
Washington, D.C. 20500

White House Comment Line: (202) 456-1111

Sample Letter

The following sample shows the essential elements of a persuasive letter to an elected representative. (Note that the numbers shown in the letter correspond to the numbered tips that follow.)

The Honorable Robert Smith
U.S. House of Representatives
Washington, D.C. 20515

Dear Representative Smith (1):

Thank you for supporting the recent House legislation to increase the minimum wage by $1 over two years (2). As you know, the debate is not over yet (3). In this critical time, I urge you to continue to push for passage of an increase in the minimum wage of at least $1 over the next two years (4).

One in ten households in the U.S. cannot afford the food their families need. In my work at Shepherd's Table in southwest Houston, I have met many hard-working families whose full-time job does not make ends meet (5). A higher minimum wage would help these families make work pay and put food on their tables.

Your leadership on these issues is very important. I look forward to working with you to help end hunger in our world.

Sincerely,

Ann McCurry
123 Stella Link
Houston, TX 77012 (6)

Tips

1. Always start with the proper title: Honorable or Representative/Senator.
2. Be brief and courteous. Many effective letters are only four or five sentences long. If you can, begin your letter by thanking your representative for a recent vote or speech that you appreciated. Check out voting records to find out about votes you favor and how elected officials have voted.
3. Time your message to be most effective. The legislative process list on page 134 (under "Time Your Message") shows at what key times to write your letters to have the most impact.
4. Be specific. Identify the particular legislative proposal you are writing about, and briefly explain why you want your representative to support or oppose it.
5. Write your own letter and personally sign it. Think about what makes you change your mind on an issue. It is not always the fact-filled argument, but a concerned person who shares his or her own experiences and observations.
6. Put your return address on the letter as well as on the envelope. Most congressional offices respond to constituent mail with a letter. Your address shows your member of Congress that you are a constituent, as either a student or a registered voter in the congressional district or state.

References

www.vote-smart.org is a nonpartisan organization that tracks voting records and contact information.

thomas.loc.gov supplies research on specific legislation. It is a service of the Library of Congress.

www.networklobby.org includes tools for lobbying Congress and local elected officials, as well as the steps to a bill becoming a law.

www.bread.org is the Web site for Bread for the World, a grassroots advocacy organization that tracks hunger-related legislation and shows how members of Congress are voting on key issucs.

www.sojo.net contains action alerts on critical issues of the day.

Advice from a Seasoned Letter-Writer

After educating ourselves as a group on the issue, we plan our letter-writing campaign about a month in advance. We set up our letter-writing table for three consecutive days, usually Monday, Tuesday, and Wednesday of the same week. We set the table outside, or just inside, a different building each day for about four hours during a popular time.

At the table, we are always sure to have plenty of paper, pens, envelopes, sample letters (which should be only a paragraph or two), clipboards, and several lists of representatives and senators by state. We make posters with facts and a sample letter around the table to attract attention to it. Making sure no one can pass the table without looking at it is key.

We always have two volunteers behind the table, coordinating and distributing the materials and answering questions. The volunteers behind the table make the letter-writing campaign run smoothly and without confusion.

We also have at least two to three volunteers in front of the table, with clipboards and paper in hand, actively approaching people. The volunteers in front of the table are crucial to getting a high number of letters. If people aren't asked to write, they most likely won't ask what's going on. An effective way to confront people is to approach confidently, with a friendly smile, explain the issue in one or two sentences, and then ask if they could take a minute to write a letter. We continuously emphasize to everyone that their letter can make a difference in the lives of hungry people. This is particularly important on campuses, since many young people don't vote because they feel that they can't make a difference.

One last piece of advice for your letter-writing campaign: Never sit! Those working the campaign are supposed to be the ones most committed to the campaign and most excited to be a part of it.

—TERRY MAMBU, VILLANOVA UNIVERSITY

MEET WITH YOUR MEMBER OF CONGRESS

Few actions can match the effectiveness of meeting with your member of Congress face to face, whether at his or her Washington office, a district office, or a community forum. Elected officials are strongly affected by the opinions of constituents who are committed enough to a specific concern to arrange a visit.

Tips

- Call your representative's appointment secretary to schedule a meeting time. Tell the scheduler what topic(s) you want to cover, and be sure to mention how many people you'll have with you. Some congressional offices are small. If you're bringing a large group, the office staff may need to prepare an alternative meeting space. Small groups are okay; you don't need to promise a crowd.
- If you're a student, organize a diverse group from your campus's congressional district to attend. Consider what may help persuade your representative. For example, if your member of Congress has a particular religious persuasion, invite prominent community leaders from that faith tradition to accompany you on the visit.
- You don't have to be a policy expert, but you do have to be well prepared. You should be conversant with the main points of the legislation you're addressing without engaging congressional staff in a heated debate. Prepare main talking points that are key to your position.
- Ask your member of Congress to take a specific action. As an active citizen, you may be tempted to bring many issues into your visit, but you will be more effective if you focus on one or two main issues in the short time you have.
- You may be told, either before or at the meeting, that you will meet with a legislative aide instead of your representative. Don't be discouraged. Aides are usually well informed and offer critical advice that will help shape the representative's position on a range of issues.
- You may have only a few minutes with the member of Congress or aide, so keep it short and stick to your talking points. If you have more time, you can discuss additional points about the issue and hear your host's views and opinions.
- After your visit, stay in touch with the office by sending a thank-you note. This is your opportunity to build a relationship with your member of Congress. Follow up in

a timely manner with any requested materials and information. If the member of Congress commits to take a specific action, keep an eye on it.

CARRY OUT A PHONE-CALLING CAMPAIGN

Sometimes legislation moves so quickly on Capitol Hill that there's no time to write letters or arrange a visit; in that case, telephone calls are a fast and personal way to express your concerns.

Tips

Call your member of Congress at his or her Washington, D.C., office. Call the Capitol switchboard at (202) 224-3121, and ask for your member.

Identify yourself and your affiliation (your school, your group, or your hometown).

Ask to speak with the member of Congress or the legislative aide handling the issue. If neither person is available, leave a message with your name, address, and phone number with the receptionist.

If you're generating numerous calls, ask callers to leave a message with the receptionist. Since you're trying to build a positive relationship with the staff, you don't want to overload the legislative aide with too many calls. A few callers can contact the aide to let him or her know that there are many messages with the receptionist about the issue.

Keep your message brief. As when writing an effective letter, be sure to make a specific request of your representative.

Be prepared to have background information on your issue available to send to the office if there are any questions. Contact organizations like Sojourners, Bread for the World, and Oxfam America that follow the issues you care about for helpful resources.

Setting Up a Phone Tree

To generate a persuasive number of calls, form a telephone-tree network of activists to pass a message along to your member of Congress at crucial times in the legislative process. Every person on the network delivers a suggested message to the congressional office. This flood of calls can sway an undecided vote or convince a legislator who wonders where the public stands on the issue.

- Choose a coordinator to maintain and activate the phone tree. This person will pass along the message to several key people, who will continue to pass the message on to other members.
- Make a list of the current phone numbers of your members.
- Select a few key people to be responsible for calling up to ten people.
- Give these key people the names and phone numbers of members to be called.
- Be sure to pass along a short and concise message. Since the message will go through the tree, it needs to be clear enough for everyone to write it down and repeat it to the congressional office.
- Keep your phone tree current and working. After the phone tree has been activated, the last person on the tree should call the coordinator to verify that the message made it through the network.

TIME YOUR MESSAGE

Whether you are conducting a letter-writing campaign, activating a phone tree, or visiting with your member of Congress, be sure to time your action to have the most impact. You can exert the most influence by taking action at these key points in the legislative process:

- Before a bill is introduced, you can help generate support for the legislation and urge your member of Congress to be a sponsor of the bill.
- When a bill is introduced, urge your representative to cosponsor it. As a cosponsor, your member of Congress can show his or her support for the bill before it comes up for a vote. A long list of both Republicans and Democrats shows broad and unified support for a bill.
- A key stage in the legislative process is when a committee or subcommittee is "marking up" the bill—that is, considering the individual provisions and making requested changes. If your member of Congress is on the committee or subcommittee, be sure to voice your opinion about provisions you would like to have removed or changed.
- When the bill goes to the House or Senate floor for a final vote, urge your members of Congress to support it or oppose it.
- For the status of the bill you are following, check out www.vote-smart.org, thomas.loc.gov, and organizational Web sites that track the issue you care about. (See "Getting Involved," the section immediately following this appendix, for a comprehensive listing of organizations.)

USE THE MEDIA

Tips

Develop and maintain a "press list" (which consists of the reporter's name, title, address, phone number, email address, fax number, and deadlines). Be sure to include wire services (Independent Media, Associated Press, Reuters), local and regional newspapers/magazines, local e-zines, local TV news and talk shows, local cable stations, and special interest publications (ethnic, college, high school, religious, punk, trade, professional).

Meet with reporters, DJs, talk-show hosts, and editors personally, to develop a relationship and establish rapport. See where their interests lie. Follow up with phone calls to give them story ideas or to give them an update on your program.

Read reporters' stories. Give them feedback—make them aware you are reading, watching, and listening to them. By reading their stories, you will know the best person to contact for your media outreach.

Be prepared to give reporters facts, accurate information, quotes, historical background information, and if possible an "exclusive," meaning they are the reporter breaking the news.

Return reporters' calls as soon as possible.

Use all the "free" resources the media offers, such as the calendar column, op-ed pieces, letters to the editor, press releases, and public service announcements.

Op-Ed Pieces

Op-ed pieces are a highly effective way of expressing your opinion in the newspaper. Op-eds are opinion pieces that appear opposite editorial pages. At their best, they are persuasive, well-thought-out, well-written, short in length (usually about 800 words) but longer than a letter to the editor, and authored by a high-profile person or someone who has experience with the issue. The op-ed should be timely and present a strong, well-informed position supported by facts.

Letters to the Editor

Letters to the editor represent your perspective in the local newspaper and can be a counter-argument for articles that you don't agree with. They also:

- Reach a large audience
- Are monitored by elected officials and other decision makers
- Create an impression of widespread support for or against an issue

The following guidelines will help you write an effective letter to the editor:

Be Direct

Make one point (or at most two) in your letter. Because letters are often edited, state the point clearly in the first paragraph. Start with a catchy opening, and use the active voice.

Be Timely

Address a specific issue of current importance, or take on an article, editorial, or letter that recently appeared in the paper you're writing to. If the latter, refer to the title, date, and author of the piece you're agreeing with or disputing.

Support Your Facts

If the topic you're addressing is controversial, consider sending documentation along with your letter—but don't overload the editors with too much information. Refute or support specific statements, address relevant facts that are ignored, and avoid attacking the reporter or the newspaper.

Find a Local Angle

Try to explain the issue's local or personal impact, to bring the issue home for readers. Look at the letters that appear in your local paper. If a certain type of letter is printed more often than others, try to follow that approach.

Know Your Audience

Familiarize yourself with the coverage and editorial position of the paper. Be professional: this is not a letter to a friend. Write for the community that reads the paper—for example, don't try to discuss technical terms if the audience won't know the technicalities of the issue.

Maximize Use of the Letter

Send the letter to neighborhood, alternative, high school, and college papers. The smaller the publication, the more likely it will get published. Get other people to write letters as well. If your letter doesn't get published, perhaps someone else's letter on the same topic will.

Pay Attention to Logistics

Check and adhere to the newspaper's letter specifications, especially regarding word limits. Write in short paragraphs (three sentences long), find out the editor's name, include your own contact information (name, address, phone number, email address), and type or email the letter.

Press Releases

A press release is a full and succinct account of your story/event, usually one or two pages, and should be written as a news article. Press releases help editors write an article. In fact, some small community newspapers will actually print your press release "as is."

- The first paragraph is the lead. In one to three sentences, it answers, "Who, what, when, where, why, and how?" The lead must grab the editor's attention.
- The second paragraph is the bridge. It names the source of the information and serves as a transition for the more detailed information.
- The third paragraph is the body. The information given in the lead is explained in detail in the body. This is the place to add quotations, facts not included in the lead, and general information on the organization.
- Finally, a photograph can be included to grab attention.

You may want to follow up any press release with a phone call and/or a personal visit. That additional contact may increase a reporter's or editor's interest in the story.

Logistics

Type the release, double-spaced, on letterhead with wide margins. At the top include the name and phone numbers for the contact person, the date and time for the story's release, and a short headline. When there is more than one page, type "–MORE–" at the bottom. The last page should conclude with "###" or "–END–." Fax the release to the newspaper's editor or to a reporter with whom you have a relationship.

Public Service Announcements

Public service announcements (PSAs) are short messages that radio and television stations air free of charge on behalf of community organizations. Contact your local public service director at the television and radio stations serving your area for the exact requirements for placing a PSA. That person may even be able to help you produce the PSA.

- Make the PSA personal and give it a sense of immediacy, remembering that PSAs are designed to be *heard*.
- Try to grab the interest and attention of the target audience.
- Use active voice and present tense when possible.
- Inform listeners/viewers how they can contact your organization—include your phone number and Web site. Be prepared for increased calls.
- Include accurate facts, dates, and names. Answer the questions, "Who, what, why, when, where, and how?"
- Read your PSA aloud. Does it read smoothly? Are the words too difficult to pronounce comfortably?

- Fit your message to the time slot: on average, 10 seconds = 25 words, 30 seconds = 75 words, 60 seconds = 150 words.
- Send a thank-you letter to the public service director and/or the DJ or TV host that airs the PSA, and ask your friends to do the same. Station personnel like positive feedback!
- If you're hoping that your PSA will engender television coverage, remember that TV stories are short and simple (usually only thirty to sixty seconds); the assignment editor often decides the day's coverage the day *before* and thus needs advance warning; and generally only events held before 3 P.M. can be covered on the day itself.

ORGANIZE A TEACH-IN

Visualize young people gathered in a church or a community center in the 1960s to listen to Howard Thurman and Martin Luther King Jr. teaching about how to organize and describing the underlying issues of racism. They were conducting what are often called "teach-ins"—probably the most successful teach-ins of the previous century. It's your turn now!

- Decide what you want to do. This will depend upon your audience and how ambitious you are. You can show a movie, invite a speaker, have a forum of students and professors, or do a workshop on a specific skill or topic. You can even do all of these things over a few days and call the result a conference. One model is to host a two-part series: at the first session you could show a video, for example, and at the second host an interactive workshop.
- Reserve a room, confirm the speakers (have a backup plan in case they don't show!), check to make sure you're not competing with a concert or other popular event, get any needed visual aids (video, flip charts, etc.), make (or order from a national organization) educational pamphlets, and get food and drinks.
- Get the word out! Why bother organizing a teach-in if no one comes? Set an attendance goal. Put up posters or write the information with chalk on sidewalks or chalkboards. Gather up your friends. Go to other meetings where people might be interested in the topic, and tell them about the teach-in. If you're on a campus, ask professors to give extra credit to students who attend the teach-in and write a paper for class.
- Create your agenda. Make your teach-in fun and interactive. Do an interesting icebreaker to get the teach-in started.
- Conduct the teach-in! Get participants' contact information to keep them informed on any next steps that develop. Offer at least one way they can immediately take action. For example, they might be able to send online faxes before they leave. (See also the earlier information about conducting a letter-writing campaign.)

Not all teach-ins go by that name. *Open mikes* and *speak-outs* are great ways to maximize young people's voices on controversial issues and to encourage them to exercise their rights to free speech. If you're a student, find out if your campus has a "free speech zone." Common areas like the cafeteria are the perfect setting. The downside to this activity is the lack of control. Having a clear message will help, but remember that you want people to express their views. Keep in mind the noise you will create, and make sure you're not disruptive to others.

Debates and *panel discussions* are a great way to get both sides of an issue aired, so make sure you truly have all points of view equally represented. In these forums, as in any type of teach-in, be respectful of opposing views.

SAMPLE
Agenda for an International Monetary Fund (IMF) Teach-In

Do introductions. Have all participants tell their first name and say one word that describes why they are at the teach-in. (10 minutes)

Check labels. Have people check the clothing label of their neighbor, looking for the country of origin. Have people describe the conditions under which they think the clothes were made. (10 minutes)

Educate. Show video introducing the IMF. Review your prepared notes on the flip chart about what "structural adjustment" is and how many countries are in debt. (20 minutes)

Break into small groups. Break into groups of four and discuss what you thought about the video and the role of the IMF. (10 minutes)

Brainstorm. Regroup and list action steps the group can take to combat the problems created by the IMF. (15 minutes)

Determine next steps. End the teach-in by having everyone write on a piece of paper one action step that he or she will take. Ask people to display their action steps at home to remind themselves of commitments made. (5 minutes)

COORDINATE A DEMONSTRATION

Young people often take an active role in planning and participating in large-scale demonstrations in Washington, D.C. Smaller demonstrations happen daily on campuses and in local communities. The book *The Future Is Ours* by John W. Bartlett suggests keeping the following in mind when deciding on what type of demonstration to hold: you *rally* for something you support, and you *protest* against something you oppose.

Consider the following types of demonstrations:

Vigil. Typically a quiet event at night with candles to honor and remember lost lives or victims. Example: Take Back the Night.

Sit-in. An event where people occupy a public or private space, typically a decision maker's office, and don't leave until a stated demand is met or negotiated. Example: a sit-in held at a university's president's office because of sweatshop labor being used to make the school's apparel (see below).

March. A group of people, holding signs and chanting, who walk from a designated point to a communal destination in order for a message to be conveyed to the public and to decision makers. Example: Million Man March.

Picket line. People, holding signs and chanting, who march outside a building or office. Example: union workers on strike.

SAMPLE
Protesting Sweatshop Labor

Putting pressure on the university administration to ban sweatshop labor from being used to produce campus products at Georgetown University in Washington, D.C., really gained momentum when a student from the university visited a factory in Latin America and saw a cap with the Georgetown logo. Student activist Michael Levinson said, "The sit-in at the president's office that we organized came after months of educating ourselves, the campus, and the administration about the issues. We won full public disclosure, meaning that we know the locations of the factories that are making Georgetown apparel. We also created a 'code of conduct' that all of our vendors must agree to follow." To date, more than eighty campuses have had similar success.

Civil Disobedience

The basic definition of civil disobedience is the refusal to obey civil laws regarded as unjust, usually by employing methods of passive resistance or by using nonviolent tactics to (indirectly) protest laws, actions, or policies—for example, by peacefully violating *other* laws. The ACLU describes civil disobedience as the vigorous public expression of controversial views. It is a cherished and vital part of American democracy, protected by the First Amendment to our Constitution. Nonviolent protest—even if unlawful—should always be met by a nonviolent response by police. For more information and ideas, check out the *Handbook for Nonviolence* by the War Resisters League.

It's important to remember that (1) all types of demonstrations require planning, and (2) a demonstration needs to be part of an overall strategy.

Tips

Core group of organizers. Assign specific roles to people, such as media representative, outreach director, permit coordinator, and publicity manager.

Turnout. Numbers are important, because the public and the media look to the number of people you can mobilize and equate that to the level of support you have for your issue. Develop a specific strategy, including a goal for the number of people you will recruit to attend the demonstration. Check out the "Get the Word Out" section (below) for ideas on recruiting people.

Permits and officials. Know your rights regarding use of space on campus or in the community. Gather all necessary permits so that the protest is not shut down for a logistical reason. Talk to the campus or community police about the demonstration. If you're planning to risk arrest, have trained legal observers at the event to take notes. The ACLU (www.aclu.org) is extremely helpful in clarifying your rights and responsibilities.

Equipment. Make sure you have everything you need (megaphones, poster board, first aid kit, tarps for rain, information flyers) and that the electrical and sound equipment works.

Press packets. Prepare folders for the press with detailed fact sheets, letters to the editor written by your group, press releases, and recommendations for a solution to the issue for which you're rallying. Make sure you include a one-pager with major points for those reporters who need a quick reference. See "Use the Media" (above) for more tips.

Slogans and chanting. Come up with catchy slogans the group can quickly learn. Get participants to chant loudly but not belligerently. Keep in mind that you want to educate, not alienate, the passersby.

Signs. Make signs that have bold letters and a clear message. Most passersby don't have the time or inclination to stop and chat with demonstrators, so it's important that your signs catch their attention and send a clear message. Once you catch someone's attention, that person is more likely to listen to the facts or hold a hand out to receive a fact sheet.

Puppets. Life-size puppets dramatize your issue and serve as a great visual for the media while the demonstration is happening.

Speakers. Gather a diverse group of people to speak, including those who are directly affected by the issue. Aim to involve young and old people, people of varying races and levels of education, and varying physical abilities (make sure they have accessibility). Give short time slots for each speaker—this is a demonstration, not a teach-in.

Timing. Hold your demonstration around a time when decision makers will be near you—for example, at a convention.

Weather. Consider a backup plan if your demonstration is scheduled to be outside. You might, for example, assign a rain date on all your flyers and promotional materials.

Visibility. Hold the demonstration where there's lots of traffic (cars or pedestrians).

Options. Consult www.interlog.com/~ksimons/198.htm for a comprehensive list of methods of nonviolent action. Give serious consideration to which method would achieve the best results for your particular issue.

TAKE CREATIVE ACTION

In today's busy world, how do you get people to stop and take notice? Creative action can be a great way to get attention and help to educate others about an issue.

Tips

Focus your creative action on a specific target and message.

Creative actions don't have to be theatrical; you can make a banner, billboard, or anything visual, for example.

Research history—the civil rights movement (Martin Luther King Jr.), nonviolent actions (Gandhi), apartheid (South Africa)—to learn more about direct action techniques already taken, including challenges and successes.

Here are some examples:

100 Chairs[2]

To demonstrate the growing wealth divide in the United States, line up 100 chairs in a high-traffic place on campus. Have 10 people spread out over 70 chairs (lying down, stretching out) while 90 people squeeze themselves onto the remaining 30 chairs. This shows that 10 percent have 70 percent of the wealth, while all the rest (90 percent) have only 30 percent of the wealth.

You can modify this exercise using 10 chairs and 10 people. You can also use this same concept to demonstrate other statistics, adjusting the number of chairs and people as needed.

Human Bar Graph[3]
Have 100 students line up to represent the president's salary, while a single person represents a janitor's salary. A sign or spokesperson explains what's represented by the human bar graph.

Interactive Theater
Create a controversial five-minute skit on some issue (for example, hunger, homelessness, racism, sexism). Act out the whole skit once for your audience. Then repeat the skit, allowing people in the audience to say "Stop" at any point. The person stopping the skit then replaces a character he or she chooses and changes the play. Hold a discussion at the end.

Guerrilla Theater
Create a dramatization that highlights your issue. For example, when Georgetown University students were protesting sweatshop labor in the production of campus wear, they staged a fashion show in a high-traffic area of campus. Students donned clothes with the university logo, and as they strutted down the walkway, the emcee talked about the substandard wages paid to workers who assembled the clothes. Guerrilla theater was often used in the 1980s to dramatize death-squad abductions in Central America: students would stage an "abduction" in the cafeteria. This creative action engaged many students in Central American solidarity work.

Invisible Theater
Create a situation that will draw onlookers into a discussion about an important issue. For example: two people go into a clothing store where sweatshop labor is being used to manufacture the clothes. The cell phone of one person rings. "Hello. Yeah, I'm here shopping at [Name of Store].... What? You're kidding! They use sweatshop labor to produce their clothes? Hey [to the second shopper, in a loud voice so that others can hear], did you know that [Name of Store] uses sweatshop labor to make their clothes?" Draw the other shoppers and staff people into a discussion of living wages as a human right.

Modeling
Make an issue real for people by modeling it in visible, physical form. For example, build shantytown housing on campus to demonstrate how people not earning a decent wage are forced to live in many countries. Sleep out in your quad to demonstrate homelessness in the United States.

References
www.sojo.net for information and alerts on budget and economic justice activities
www.faireconomy.org for information on a campus living wage campaign
www.globalexchange.org for updates on boycotts and demonstrations
www.coopamerica.org for listings of ethical companies and boycotts

INITIATE CYBER-ACTIVISM

Activists today have a tool that the previous generation didn't: the Internet. Savvy computer users can use the Internet to help them organize an event, disseminate information, and contact their representatives.

Rallying a Large Group of People for an Event (Virtual Organizing)

As the November 1999 Seattle WTO and the April 2000 IMF/World Bank protests showed, the Internet can be an extremely powerful organizing tool.

Tips

Create a Web page to go with your event. Make your emails short, and direct people to a hyperlink to the Web for more details. Make sure your page is always up-to-date.

Find a service provider that allows people to easily subscribe to your listserv (try groups .yahoo.com or groups.msn.com).

Creating a Listserv/Electronic Mailing List

A listserv is a single email address that actually contains your "list" of email addresses. Listservs are a way to discuss issues, organize, and share ideas and resources with a group of people. You can create your own (for your particular event/cause) and also join existing ones to keep up on the issues. Make sure to actively collect email addresses at all your events, and use your listserv to keep activists informed and connected.

Find out more by looking at these cyber-activist Web sites with resources for virtual organizing:

www.netaction.org/training/, which offers NetAction's virtual activist training reader
www.afj.org, Alliance for Justice, which offers e-advocacy for nonprofits
www.organizenow.net, which offers technology and training to advance and sustain social change

Creating connections among the local activists in your city/town can be an important way to sustain you in your work. Check out www.idealist.org to search for the activists near you. Get together and support each other in your work. This can be a great social network as well!

Lobbying Your Representative Online

Even though most representatives have email addresses and even Web pages, legislators usually respond better to the traditional lobbying tactics of visits, letters, phone calls, faxes, and postcards. It's best to experiment with a variety of tactics to see which works with your representative(s).

When you send an email to your representative, always include your mailing address in your email. Many emails will be taken seriously only if you include your physical address, because that's the only way a legislator knows you're in his or her district.

Take a look at "Conduct a Letter-Writing Campaign" (above). An effective email letter should follow the same guidelines as a snail-mail letter.

Use the following Web sites for information on how to contact your federal, state, and local representatives:

www.senate.gov to contact the U.S. Senate

www.house.gov to contact the U.S House of Representatives

thomas.loc.gov to contact the Library of Congress

www.vote-smart.org to access a nonpartisan organization that tracks voting records, campaign finance information, issue positions, performance evaluations, and contact information

FINANCE YOUR ACTIVIST PROJECTS

Money—we all need it for the activities we want to organize. Often activists are called the "out-of-pocket" sector because we use our own money to fund our projects. However, there are ways to fund activism without going broke!

Tips

Check with activist organizations in your community and with national and international nonprofits and businesses. Often they have funds to support a specific issue. They can at least send you free educational materials to distribute at your event.

Look up foundations on the Web. There are many that support young people and activists. For example, check out www.foundationcenter.org.

If you're a student, try to get funds from your campus—perhaps from the student activity center, student government, or the political science department (or other departments relevant to your issue). Make a pitch to the university committee that plans speakers and alumni events.

Hold a fundraiser. Make it fun. Have a theme party, cookout, house party, rave, talent show, or car wash. Check out www.alternativebreaks.com for other great ideas.

GET THE WORD OUT

Publicity is a key element in the success of any campaign. Build a movement by educating people about your issue and then mobilizing them to join your events. Be consistent, frequent, and creative with your marketing tactics.

Tips

Create a core concept that can be expressed in seven words and put it on everything you publish. For example, a group of young people working on body image and eating disorders came up with "Mobilizing young people to eliminate eating disorders."

Make up baseball cards with the "villains" or "heroes" of the movement, and include statistics, facts, and interesting information about the people on the cards.

Write personal letters to people inviting them to participate, telling them the specific skills they possess and how those skills could be used in the project.

Use chalk on sidewalks, streets, and chalkboards to advertise an event or message.

Run a classified advertisement with the heading, "Looking for Activists."

Create a controversial billboard ad.

Post your flyers on community billboards, corporate bulletin boards, and/or nonprofit bulletin boards.

If you're a student, ask professors and teachers if you can speak for two minutes before or after a class.

Get a magazine to run an ad for you. This requires relationship building.

Ask the campus and community radio and TV stations to run a PSA.

Run your campaign in waves. The first week you put up posters with one line or symbol. The next week you add on to that line or symbol. The next week you add on to the previous week. By the fourth week the flyer should convey a complete message.

Create a symbol that represents your movement; then make stickers incorporating that symbol, and post them everywhere.

Post your flyers in restaurants and bars, always asking permission first.

Make up buttons and bumper stickers, and hand them out.

Produce T-shirts with your message and Web address—make them funny or controversial.

Give away compact disks with a label that has your message and Web address.

Use the Internet—emails, banner ads, and pop-up messages.

Hand out flyers, T-shirts, bumper stickers, or posters—all with your message and Web site—at a concert.

Ask a store if you can use their window for a display on your issue and/or event.

You know those free postcard stands at restaurants and coffee shops? Get a postcard printed for your issue—it's not expensive.

For protests, get rain parkas made up with your message on the back.

Order fortune cookies that have your message or facts about your issue inside.

When ordering T-shirts, stickers, business cards, or any promotional material, consider having the articles union-made to ensure that they aren't made using sweatshop labor. Check out www.unitehere.org (click on "buy union") for a resource in your community.

Use Flyers

Flyers are expected and necessary tools of publicity. They can be used creatively, consistently, and frequently. In preparation for the Oxfam Hunger Banquet at one university, students hung colorful flyers with simple, catchy phrases that conveyed their most immediate message in order to gain the attention of lots of casual passersby. Doors and walls along stairwells are typically excellent spots because it's hard to dismiss flyers when they're hung at eye level. Students can also hang informative flyers in bathroom stalls, on bulletin boards, near drinking fountains, in the library lobby, and near tables at the student union. Consistency and use of your campus's unique resources will help ensure that you've reached many people.

Flyers are a great chance to inform and convince people of the importance of your issue with thoughtful and creative art and words. They might include pictures, tables, graphs, copied articles, and a collage of facts—anything with the potential to really move the reader.

Plan Ahead and Follow Through

Be sure to plan ahead and follow through. Three weeks before the Oxfam Hunger Banquet mentioned above, the sponsoring organization announced the date, time, and place of its upcoming event. They had a representative attend the student government's weekly meetings to publicize; and they advertised through the Residence Life Office, which may require student RAs and hall counselors to decorate bulletin boards or plan educational and service hall programs. Asking these students, and other organizations like fraternities, sororities, and health- and gender-related student groups, to post information or promote an event can really increase participation. Cosponsoring events and pooling funds with other student organizations to bring a high-profile guest speaker to the campus or community can also result in successful events and memorable experiences.

Be Creative

Effective publicity usually means attracting the optimal number of participants. To do this, creative advertising that draws a diverse and large crowd is recommended. As an example, to gain attention for an upcoming international festival on campus, the hosting organization obtained school permission to borrow golf carts and play music as organizers safely drove around campus passing out flyers between scheduled class times. This creative approach grabbed the attention of many.

Getting Involved

Now that you've read this book, we encourage you to become involved in your community. Here are some organizations that are active around the country and provide information on how you can become involved. They cover the political spectrum, and many of them address multiple issues discussed in this book.

> Sojourners/Call to Renewal
> 3333 14th Street NW, Suite 200
> Washington, DC 20010
> Phone: (202) 328-8842 or (800) 714-7474
> Fax: (202) 328-8757
> Web site: www.sojo.net and www.calltorenewal.org
> e-mail: sojourners@sojo.net and ctr@calltorenewal.org

For free regular updates, please sign up for the SojoMail e-zine at www.sojo.net.

Sojourners and Call to Renewal share an overarching statement of mission: to articulate the biblical call to social justice, inspiring hope and building a movement to transform individuals, communities, the church, and the world.

Sojourners, established in 1971, is a nonprofit organization whose mission is to offer a voice and vision for social change. Sojourners attracts a diverse group of evangelicals, Catholics, and Protestant Christians, as well as others who are united on issues of justice and peace.

Call to Renewal is a national network of churches, faith-based organizations, and individuals working to overcome poverty in America. Through local and national partnerships with groups from across the theological and political spectrum, Call to Renewal convenes the broadest table of Christians focused on antipoverty efforts.

The Covenant for a New America is a policy platform intended to move beyond the debate between Left and Right by seeking to create a common commitment to identify, pursue, and bring about real solutions to poverty. The covenant lifts up both personal and social responsibility with policies that address the individual decisions and social systems that trap people in poverty. It identifies policies that move beyond looking solely to charity or only to government. It acknowledges that budgets are moral documents and that budget priorities can help or hurt poor people—and that negative family and cultural values also impact low-income people.

A combination of policies in four major areas will allow the covenant's vision to engage concretely with the policymaking process. We seek changes that will promote (1) a living family income for all who work; (2) the rebuilding of neighborhoods and communities; (3) the strengthening of families and the renewing of culture; and (4) an end to extreme global poverty.

For more information, see www.covenantforanewamerica.org. Sojourners/Call to Renewal is launching a new congregational network aimed at empowering, resourcing, and connecting clergy and laity interested in issues of social justice, peace, and spiritual renewal. A variety of resources for preaching, teaching, and issue advocacy, as well as discounts on Sojourner's/Call to Renewal conferences and events, will be included in the network offering. We are excited to be able to provide these tools and would like to offer you the chance to get in on the ground floor. To find out more and to receive announcements about the rollout of the program, please indicate your interest by going to www.sojo.net/network and providing your contact information.

In addition, consider the following organizations, listed in alphabetical order:

Asset-Based Development Institute. Provides resources and tools for communities and governments involved in capacity-based development initiatives.
(847) 491-8711   http://www.northwestern.edu/ipr/abcd.html

Bread for the World. A nationwide Christian citizens' movement seeking justice for the world's hungry people by lobbying our nation's decision makers.
(202) 639-9400   www.bread.org

Catholic Charities USA. Works to reduce poverty, support families, and empower communities by providing for people in need and advocating for justice.
(703) 549-1390   www.catholiccharitiesusa.org

Center for Public Justice. An independent organization for policy research and civic education whose mission is to equip citizens, develop leaders, and shape policy.
(866) 275-8784   http://www.cpjustice.org

Children's Defense Fund. Works through education and advocacy to ensure every child a healthy, fair, safe, and moral start in life for successful passage to adulthood.
(202) 628-8787   www.childrensdefense.org

Christian Community Development Association. A nationwide network of grassroots community-based organizations working to provide social and spiritual service to those in poverty.
(773) 762-0994   www.ccda.org

Christian Peacemaker Teams. Promotes biblically based and spiritually centered peacemaking and emphasizes creative public witness, nonviolent direct action, and protection of human rights.
(773) 277-0253   www.cpt.org

Church World Service. The relief, development, and refugee assistance ministry of thirty-five Protestant, Orthodox, and Anglican denominations in the United States.
(800) 297-1516   www.churchworldservice.org

Direct Action and Research Training Center (DART). A national network of community-organizing efforts, many of which are congregation-based.
(305) 576-8020   www.thedartcenter.org

EMU Center for Justice and Peacebuilding. An organization founded to further the personal and professional development of individuals as peacebuilders.
(540) 432-4490   http://www.emu.edu/ctp

Equal Exchange. Offers fair-trade coffee, tea, and chocolate through partnerships with faith communities and congregations.

(774) 776-7400   www.equalexchange.com

Evangelical Environmental Network. An evangelical ministry whose purpose is to "declare the Lordship of Christ over all creation"; published the 1994 "Evangelical Declaration on the Care of Creation," a manifesto seeking to relate biblical faith to environmental problems.

(202) 554-1955   http://www.creationcare.org

Evangelicals for Social Action. Promotes a lifestyle marked by service to poor and powerless people, reverence for life, care for creation, and witness to Jesus Christ.

(610) 645-9390   www.esa-online.org

Families Against Violence Advocacy Network. A broad-based network of organizations, families, and individuals committed to promoting alternatives to violence.

(314) 918-2630   http://www.ipj-ppj.org

Gamaliel Foundation. A national network of community-organizing efforts, many of which are congregation-based.

(312) 357-2639   www.gamaliel.org

Habitat for Humanity. Brings families and communities in need together with volunteers and resources to build decent, affordable housing through a national network of affiliates.

(912) 924-6935   www.habitat.org

Industrial Areas Foundation. A national network of community-organizing efforts, many of which are congregation-based.

(312) 245-9211   http://www.industrialareasfoundation.org

Interfaith Center for Corporate Responsibility. Works through education, organizing, and stockholder resolutions to promote more socially responsible actions by corporations.

(212) 870-2295   www.iccr.org

Interfaith Worker Justice. Works to educate and organize the faith community in the United States on issues and campaigns to benefit workers.

(773) 728-8400   www.iwj.org

International Justice Mission. A human rights agency that rescues victims of violence, sexual exploitation, slavery, and oppression.

(703) 465-5495   http://www.ijm.org

Jesuit Volunteer Corps. A Catholic lay-volunteer program whose individuals work in grassroots organizations across the country to provide services to low-income people.

(202) 687-1132   www.jesuitvolunteers.org

Jubilee 2000 USA. Works as part of an international campaign to educate and advocate for debt cancellation for the world's poorest countries.

(202) 783-3566   www.jubileeusa.org

Lutheran Volunteer Corps. Provides one-year service terms in urban social-justice organizations and promotes simplicity and community living as part of that commitment.

(202) 387-3222   http://www.lutheranvolunteercorps.org

Mennonite Central Committee. A relief, service, development, and peace agency working in fifty-eight countries among people suffering from poverty, conflict, and natural disaster.

(717) 859-1151   www.mcc.org

Micah Challenge. A global Christian campaign working to deepen our engagement with the poor and to challenge leaders to achieve the Millennium Development Goals.
www.micahchallenge.org

Mission Year. Offers Christian young adults a one-year term of living and serving in a poor inner-city neighborhood alongside a solid local church.
(773) 847-8856   www.missionyear.org

National Association of Evangelicals. Works to extend the kingdom of God through a fellowship of member denominations, churches, organizations, and individuals; published the 2004 "For the Health of the Nation," an evangelical call to social responsibility.
(719) 268-8214   www.nae.net

National Coalition of Barrios Unidos. Works to prevent youth violence in urban neighborhoods and promotes "gang truces," community development, and employment.
(831) 457-8208   http://www.barriosunidos.net

National Conference of Catholic Bishops/United States Catholic Conference, Department of Social Development and World Peace. The national public policy agency of the Catholic bishops.
(202) 541-3000   www.usccb.org/sdwp

National Congress of Community Economic Development. A faith-based initiative that works to promote and facilitate faith-based community economic development.
(202) 289-9020   www.ncced.org

National Living Wage Resource Center (ACORN). Provides a clearinghouse of information and resources on living wage campaigns around the country.
(718) 246-7900, x230   www.livingwagecampaign.org

NetWork. A national Catholic social justice lobby that educates and organizes to influence the formation of federal legislation to promote economic and social justice.
(202) 347-9797   www.networklobby.org

Network 9:35. A collaborative fellowship working to nurture and strengthen congregations, pastors, and leaders who are committed to holistic ministry.
(610) 645-9390   http://www.network935.org

One Campaign. An effort by Americans to rally Americans—*one* by *one*—to fight the emergency of global AIDS and extreme poverty.
www.one.org

Pacific Institute for Community Organization (PICO). A national network of community-organizing efforts, many of which are congregation-based.
(510) 655-2801   http://www.piconetwork.org

Pax Christi USA. The national Catholic peace movement that strives to create a world that reflects the peace of Christ by exploring, articulating, and witnessing to the call of Christian non-violence.
(814) 453-4955   http://www.paxchristiusa.org

Prison Fellowship. Works to provide a biblical and comprehensive assault on crime through in-prison programs and programs with children of prisoners and victims of crime.
(800) 206-9764   www.pfm.org

Public Campaign. A nonpartisan organization dedicated to reform that aims to dramatically reduce the role of special interest money in America's elections.
(202) 293-0202   www.publicampaign.org

Pura Vida Coffee. Fair-trade coffee organization rooted in a desire to empower the poor in coffee-growing regions of the world.

(877) 469-1431   www.puravidacoffee.com

Salvation Army. Affiliates across the country providing a wide range of social, medical, educational, and other community services.

(703) 684-5500   www.salvationarmy.org

United for a Fair Economy. Works to educate and organize on the dangers of the growing income, wage, and wealth inequality in the United States.

(617) 423-2148   www.faireconomy.org

Volunteers of America. A national nonprofit, spiritually based organization providing local human service programs and opportunities for individual and community involvement.

(800) 899-0089   http://www.voa.org

World Relief. Equips churches and communities to help victims of war, poverty, disease, hunger, disasters, and persecution.

(443) 451-1900   www.wr.org

World Vision. An international partnership of Christians seeking to follow Jesus Christ through working in relief and development programs with the poor and oppressed.

(253) 815-1000   www.worldvision.org

Notes

Week Two: War and Peace

1. Ron Suskind, "Without a Doubt," *The New York Times,* Oct. 17, 2004, sec. 6, p. 44.
2. *Merriam-Webster* Online, www.m-w.com.
3. http://www.whitehouse.gov/news/releases/2005/12/20051214-1.html.
4. "Iraq Body Count: A Dossier of Civilian Casualties 2003–2005," http://reports.iraqbodycount .org/a_dossier_of_civilian_casualties_2003-2005.pdf.
5. See Lee Griffiths, *The War on Terrorism and the Terror of God* (Grand Rapids, MI: Eerdmans, 2002).
6. Adapted from Glen Stassen, ed., *Just Peacemaking: Ten Practices for Abolishing War,* 2nd ed. (Cleveland, OH: Pilgrim Press, 2004).
7. Ca. 160, Alexander Roberts and James Donaldson, *The Ante-Nicene Fathers (ANF)* 1.176 (Peabody, MA: Hendrickson, 1994). In several of our discussions for Day 4 of the different weeks, we will examine the writings of the early church. For the most part, these are writings on Christian faith from the first five or so centuries of the church. Because the Christian tradition has recognized the important contributions that this group of writings has made to the development of the church and its expression of its faith, the writers were identified as "fathers" of the church.
8. Ca. 180, *ANF* 1.512.
9. Ca. 195, *ANF* 2.234; ca. 195, *ANF* 2.581.
10. Ca. 197, *ANF* 3.154.
11. Ca. 200, *ANF* 3.73.
12. Ca. 211, *ANF* 3.100.
13. Ca. 200, *Apostolic Tradition* 16.17–19.
14. Ca. 248, *ANF* 4.558.
15. See Stassen, ed., *Just Peacemaking.*

Week Three: Economic Justice

1. "Transcript: O'Neill on Enron Mess," Fox News, January 13, 2002. http://www.foxnews .com/story/0,2933,42952,00.html.
2. From www.afsc.org/economic-justice/LearnAbout.htm.
3. "For the Health of the Nation," National Association of Evangelicals, 2005. http://www.nae .net/images/civic_responsibility2.pdf.
4. *Centesimus Annus,* no. 35.
5. *Centesimus Annus,* no. 35.
6. See www.afsc.org/economic-justice/LearnAbout.htm.

7. http://www.globalpolicy.org/socecon/inequal/2005/10compendium.pdf.
8. http://www.faireconomy.org/research/wealth_charts.html.
9. http://www.faculty.fairfield.edu/faculty/hodgson/Courses/so11/stratification/income&wealth.htm.
10. Ched Myers, "Behold, the Treasure of the Church," *Sojourners,* Sept./Oct. 1999, vol. 28, no. 5, p. 33.
11. For further reading, consider Ron Sider's *For They Shall Be Fed* (Dallas: Word, 1997).
12. http://www.coady.stfx.ca/resources/publications/publications_coadylectures_notes.html.
13. http://thewitness.org/agw/gillett.html.
14. *De Nabuthe Jezraelita* 3, 11, cited in http://thewitness.org/archive/may2000/may.reuther.html.
15. *Second Sermon,* St. John Chrysostom, "Seven Sermons on Wealth and Poverty," www.byzantines.net/byzcathculture/wealth.html.
16. Sabbath Economics Collaborative, http://www.sabbatheconomics.org.
17. The Bartimeus Covenant Investors Community (http://www.bcm-net.org/page4/covenant_investment.html) provides substantial information on investing for justice.

Week Four: Poverty

1. "Ah, you who make iniquitous decrees, who write oppressive statutes, to turn aside the needy from justice and to rob the poor of my people of their right, that widows may be your spoil, and that you may make the orphans your prey! What will you do on the day of punishment, in the calamity that will come from far away? To whom will you flee for help, and where will you leave your wealth, so as not to crouch among the prisoners or fall among the slain? For all this his anger has not turned away; his hand is stretched out still."
2. See http://www.nccp.org/pub_cpf04.html.
3. Ron Sider, *Just Generosity* (Grand Rapids, MI: Baker Books, 1999), p. 20.
4. United for a Fair Economy, http://www.faireconomy.org/research/wealth_charts.html.
5. www.ccel.org/ccel/richardson/fathers.viii.i.iii.html.
6. www.apuritansmind.com/Stewardship/EarlyChurchWealth.htm.
7. www.apuritansmind.com/Stewardship/EarlyChurchWealth.htm.
8. www.apuritansmind.com/Stewardship/EarlyChurchWealth.htm.

Week Five: A Consistent Ethic of Life

1. Joseph Cardinal Bernardin, "A Consistent Ethic of Life: An American-Catholic Dialogue" (Dec. 6, 1983), http://www.hnp.org/publications/hnpfocus/BConsistentEthic1983.pdf.
2. See Tobias Winright, "Executing the Innocent," *Sojourners,* Aug. 2005, vol. 34, no. 8, p. 42.
3. David Cortright, "Hiroshima, Nagasaki, and Nuclear Realism," SojoMail, Aug. 9, 2005.
4. Stanley K. Henshaw, Susheela Singh, and Taylor Haas, "The Incidence of Abortion Worldwide," *Family Perspectives,* vol. 25, supplement, January 1999.
5. www.guttmacher.org/presentations/abort_slides.ppt.
6. Richard C. Dieter, "Misspent Millions," http://www.deathpenaltyinfo.org/article.php?scid=45&did=385#sxn1.
7. See Dr. David P. Gushee, "The Sanctity of Life: An Evangelical Exploration," http://www.uu.edu/programs/pew/Pew%20Application%20Gushee%202005.pdf.
8. Stanley Hauerwas and William H. Willimon, *Resident Aliens* (Nashville, TN: Abingdon Press, 1989).
9. Amy Sullivan, "Abortion: A Way Forward," *Sojourners,* Apr. 2006, vol. 35. no. 4, p. 15.
10. Sullivan, "Abortion," p. 15.

11. See the Supreme Court's opinion at http://www.tourolaw.edu/patch/Roe/.

12. Bernardin, "A Consistent Ethic of Life."

Week Six: Racism

1. Jim Wallis, *America's Original Sin* (Washington, DC: Sojourners, 1992), p. 8.

2. See *Exclusion and Embrace: A Theological Exploration of Identity, Otherness, and Reconciliation* (Nashville, TN: Abingdon Press, 1996).

3. See *White Theology: Outing Supremacy in Modernity* (New York: Palgrave Macmillan, 2004).

4. The percentages add up to more than 100 percent due to some overlap. For example, the Census Bureau indicates that Hispanic or Latino respondents can be "of any race." The goal is to give a general idea of the disparities that exist in incarceration rates, for example, and the percentages that given groups constitute of the overall U.S. population. For more precise numbers, go to the Census Bureau Web site at http://www.census.gov/prod/cen2000/dp1/2kh00.pdf.

5. *Sojourners,* Mar./Apr. 2000, vol. 29, no. 2, p. 10.

6. The following data are a summary from the Census Bureau via http://www.infoplease.com/ipa/A0104552.html. For a more detailed breakdown, see http://www.census.gov/hhes/www/income/income.html.

7. Data taken from http://www.census.gov/hhes/www/poverty/histpov/hstpov2.html.

8. See James Ferguson, "Double Standard," *Sojourners,* Apr. 2006, vol. 35, no. 4, p. 10.

9. Data compiled by Human Rights Watch. For more details, visit www.hrw.org/backgrounder/usa/incarceration/.

10. http://www.sentencingproject.org/issues_07.cfm.

11. http://www.sentencingproject.org/pdfs/5077.pdf.

12. www.deathpenaltyinfo.org/article.php?scid=5&did=184.

13. Jim Wallis, "America's Original Sin," *Sojourners,* Mar./Apr. 1998, vol. 27, no. 2, p. 9.

14. Bill Wylie-Kellermann, "Exorcising an American Demon: Racism Is a Principality," *Sojourners,* Mar./Apr. 1998, vol. 27, no. 2, p. 17.

15. Wylie-Kellermann, "Exorcising an American Demon."

16. See, for example, Myers's books *Binding the Strong Man* (Maryknoll, NY: Orbis Books, 1988) and *Who Will Roll Away the Stone?* (Maryknoll, NY: Orbis Books, 1994).

17. Wylie-Kellermann, "Exorcising an American Demon."

18. Martin Luther King Jr., "I Have a Dream" (1963) from *A Testament of Hope* (New York: Harper & Row, 1986), p. 219.

19. http://whatsaiththescripture.com/Voice/Revival.Lectures.4.html#LECTURE%2015.

20. http://wesley.nnu.edu/john_wesley/evangelist/JWE-12.htm.

21. In the following, we are indebted to David Gushee.

22. See www.uu.edu/centers/christld/morall/v1n3.htm.

23. *David Walker's Appeal, in Four Articles: Together with a Preamble to the Coloured Citizens of the World, but in Particular, and Very Expressly, to Those of the United States of America,* rev. ed., with introduction by Sean Wilentz (New York: Hill & Wang, 1995), http://www.pbs.org/wgbh/aia/part4/4h2931t.html.

24. Henry Highland Garnet, "Call to Rebellion," 1843, found at http://startribune.com/dynamic/story.php?template=print_a&story=646719.

25. Sojourner Truth, *"Ain't I a Woman"*; see www.sojournertruth.org/Library/Speeches/Default.htm.

Week Seven: **Strengthening Family and Community Values**

1. www.censusscope.org/us/chart_house.html.
2. The online Barna report is no longer posted, but a summary of statistics can be found at http://www.religioustolerance.org/chr_dira.htm; and commentary from *Christianity Today* can be found at http://www.christianitytoday.com/ct/2000/010/30.47.html. You will note that the *CT* article places the 1999 national divorce rate at around 25 percent, but these numbers are highly disputed and largely dependent upon definitions. Some estimate that divorce rates could be as high as 50 percent, for example. The Barna numbers are intended to remind us, as people of faith, that we have not done a good job of "practicing what we preach."
3. *Wall Street Journal,* July 14, 2005.
4. Yonce Shelton, "Budgets, Social Security, and the Common Good," http://www.sojo.net/index.cfm?action=sojomail.display&issue=050719#2.
5. S. Scott Bartchy, "Secret Siblings," *Sojourners,* Nov. 2004, vol. 33, no. 11, p. 32.
6. Ellen T. Armour, "Christian 'Family Values' Have Changed Throughout History," www.sojo.net/index.cfm?action=news.display_archives&mode=point_of_view&article=POV_050202_armour.
7. See http://www.americancatholic.org/Newsletters/VAT/aq1004.asp.
8. "Family Values, Christian Values," *Christian Century,* Jan. 31, 1996, cover story; http://www.findarticles.com/p/articles/mi_m1058/is_n4_v113/ai_17907603.
9. www.littlegeneva.com/?m=200210.
10. Armour, "Christian 'Family Values' Have Changed Throughout History."
11. http://shilohflc.org/programs.html.

Week Eight: **Hope for the Future**

1. www.wfu.edu/~matthetl/perspectives/four.html.

A Summary of Social Activism Techniques

1. Adapted from "Guide to Social Consciousness," Oxfam America. Used by permission.
2. United for a Fair Economy. www.faireconomy.org/activist/creative/popular_theater.html.
3. United for a Fair Economy. www.faireconomy.org/activist/creative/popular_theater.html.

Acknowledgments

When we began to see how many local churches and small book groups were studying the hardback version of *God's Politics*, we realized how many more might want to do the same when the paperback version came out. It was then that the idea of a companion volume emerged to help those small groups and provide more resources for study, reflection, and response.

I want to thank my publisher, Mark Tauber, and my editor, Eric Brandt, at HarperSanFrancisco for supporting and shaping the idea. But most of all, I want to thank Chuck Gutenson, an extraordinary Asbury Theological Seminary professor who spent a year with us at Sojourners to help shape our capacity to resource the churches. Chuck is a theologian, an educator, and a fine writer. After many conversations, he suggested a framework for *Living God's Politics* as a study guide and began the drafting. Then Duane Shank became involved, as he always does, and finally the *Sojourners* magazine editorial staff, especially Jim Rice and Rose Berger, did the final editing. With help like that it was easy for me to be involved all along the way. This was truly a team effort and we hope it aids your study, shapes your reflection, and guides your action.

Jim Wallis
July 2006

Notes

Notes

Notes

Notes

Notes